CANADIAN SHORTS II

A Collection of Short Stories
featuring established and
emerging Canadian authors.

MISCHIEVOUS
BOOKS

Canadian Shorts II: A Collection of Short Stories

Copyright © 2020 Mischievous Books
mischievousbooks.com

Stories copyright by the individual authors

Cover design & layout: Brenda Fisk
Editor: Brenda Fisk

ISBNs: 978-1-988829-12-8 (5x8 paperback)
978-1-988829-17-3 (6x9 large print version)
978-1-988829-13-5 (electronic book version)
978-1-988829-14-2 (eBook - Smashwords edition)

PERMISSIONS

The following authors have granted
permission for their works to appear
in this publication.

DEDICATION

This book is dedicated to
911 emergency dispatchers,
the *first,* first responders.

CONTENTS

FOREWORD

This collection of short stories by Canadian authors showcases some of the amazing talent Canada has to offer and I am delighted to be included. While everyone deals with the overwhelming difficulties of Covid-19, I would like to express my deep gratitude to all the first responders. My special thanks go to those unseen, and often unmentioned, emergency dispatchers who start the response process.

As a paramedic in emergency medical services (EMS) in Alberta, I was privileged to work with first responders throughout my career. I found that, in this emotionally demanding field, they are consistently kind, considerate and dedicated professionals with a deep desire to help people. Later in my career, as Communications Manager, I developed a specific kinship to the often overlooked *first,* first responders: the emergency dispatchers who answer your 911 call.

Emergency dispatchers are exposed to many traumatic events in the daily scope of their jobs. This psychological burden can build and affect all aspects of a person's life. It can become overwhelming without help.

Very few people understand the difficulties dispatchers encounter. I wrote The Weight of Lives as an example of how the job can overpower and overwhelm. It's about understanding when you need to seek assistance before it's too late, as well as a glimpse into the mind of those who are always there to help.

Thank you for reading.

Stacey O'Sullivan, M.A., B.A.,
Paramedic-retired

THE WEIGHT OF LIVES
by Stacey O'Sullivan

My job is to help people on the worst day of their lives. I am the voice in the night that supports them when they call me with their pain, their fear and their anger. As soon as the phone rings, my computer instantly hones in on their location and, with the push of a button, help is on the way. I am a dispatcher in an emergency communications centre.

My scripted words ensure I miss nothing. I can handle any emergency, artificial respiration, electrocution, even childbirth. I dispatch an ambulance while typing call details.

Father collapsed and is not responding.

"Paramedics are coming as fast as they can," I reassure the panicked voice on the line.

Will we arrive in time? Will they survive? I rarely know the answer and, after the first few years, each 911 phone call bled into the next.

My right-hand monitor lights up and one more frantic voice is on the line. The cycle repeats until the end of my shift, each call adding to the weight of those before—the weight of lives I carry. They are layers of trauma stacked one on top of another, a mason bricking stone into a dungeon.

My shift ends and the night air is bitterly cold as I walk across the parking lot, hoar frost clings to branches and wind swirls crystals of ice. Souls I have touched in my last twelve hours writhe in the frosty air, surround me, stifle me. I gasp and lurch to my car, pant until my breathing slows.

At home, slumped in my chair, the stew of ugliness simmers in my belly. Coffee mug clenched in my fists, I wish the heat would warm my chilled heart. Tears burn through my closed lids. I thrust back the screaming memories to make pancakes.

My family stumbles from sleep, rubbing their eyes, yawning circles of protest at the early hour. I can't let them know what's in my head. It would terrify them.

"How was your shift, Honey?" my wife asks, too busy making the kids' lunches to notice the wet streak down my cheek.

"Fine," I lie. "Same as always." We converse as though nothing at all happened overnight.

"Have a good day at school, kids," I say, handing them their lunches. The second they're out the door my smile drops from my face, I can't hold it any longer.

"Love you," I mumble and kiss my wife's cheek before she leaves for work.

Finally, everyone is gone. I trudge to the bedroom, where sunlight peeks cheerfully through the blinds, taunting me with what I miss. In the silence of the empty house, I bury my face in my pillow. Last night's calls reverberate as I stare at the slowly rotating fan and shuffle emergency events like playing cards.

Queen of Diamonds: massive heart attack.

Jack of Spades: gunshot wound to the chest.

Ace of Hearts: my child isn't breathing.

This is the poker game no one wins.

Like a rain-washed sky, the colour has been leached from my life. I now live in a monochromatic world. It wasn't sudden. Once I was young and eager, a fresh spirit with dreams for a beautiful life. I wanted to help people, to make lives better, one event at a time. It seemed like an honourable career, but that was a thousand screaming voices ago.

My alarm shrieks and I claw my way from tangled sheets. I can't even remember the last time I slept well. In the mirror, exhaustion tattoos my features. Drawn and pasty, I look older than I am. My routine is robotic. I'm an automaton with only the semblance of humanity. All those lives I've touched have melded into a tarry pool of broken bones, car crashes and death, but I still *need* to know what happened.

I flick on the TV news and there's a crime scene with a yellow tarp draped over a body. This is the same event that repeated itself in today's nightmares. Standing with yet another cup of coffee, I freeze, riveted. Bile rises in my throat. I'm an addict and this is my drug.

My children tumble into the house, bright and cheerful, eager to tell me about their day. I choke down my own sick need and turn off the TV to protect them.

I fix my smile in place while I look at their

school work. "How was your day, sweetie? That's great, honey." Is that the appropriate feedback? I don't know anymore.

The children's chatter continues, but I am back in the shadowy space in my skull, staring at the blank TV screen, where the image of the yellow tarp is etched in my memory.

My daughter bristles and her hurt brims over in tears. "I just told you I have to go to soccer practice. Aren't you listening to me?"

"Sorry, honey. Want a cookie?" I give her a one-armed hug and reassure her with a snack. She seems to be satisfied by what little I can give.

I'm frozen inside, my emotions trapped behind sheets of ice. I can't free them. Somewhere behind my torment lingers my love for my family. I pound it with my fists, but cannot break through.

My wife breezes in, smelling of winter frost and cinnamon. I used to love the way she smelled, the tiny freckles across her nose. Her lips barely brush my cheek when I turn away from her kiss. I can't look her in the eye. I can't reach out to her. She will know what I'm feeling and she can't help me. Heartache concealed behind her smile is a match for my own. We are on separate life rafts pulling away from each other, both victims of our sinking relationship. I wish we could buoy each other, but no one can reach me, least of all her. Her love is a gift I struggle to receive and her pain pushes me deeper into my gloom.

I stammer when I try to explain the toll this job takes. Few understand, my wife least of all. I can't tell anyone about the things I can't forget, lest they too are forced to carry this awful weight. I can't release the hurt and suffering from people I've never met. I am filled with their anguish. Each call shovels more ugliness and pain until I am buried in despair.

The junkie in me turns on the TV again and now the suicide of another first responder is in the news. My coffee mug slides from shaking fingers and my knees give way. I'm on the floor, stunned. I knew him. He was my friend. He was a beautiful soul in a dark world. I can't stop sobbing. I will never get his smart-assed messages again. I loved his dramatic flair and his amazing humour. He was so much more than the cold announcer states.

What about his friends and his family? What will we all do without him? What happened? Grief extinguishes my last flicker of hope.

He found *his* solution to the problem no one else understands—but it is so absolute. Didn't he have any other options? Why did he stay in this job? Why didn't he talk to someone, talk to me? Do I agree with his decision? I don't know. I can commiserate about what leads to this gloomy pathway that haunts us all. Has *my* existence become untenable?

As I leave for my last night shift, I mumble a prayer, whether for him or me, I'm not sure. My route to work is a series of mind-numbing traffic delays. Horns blare. An ambulance winds a serpentine path through the tangle of vehicles, their sirens harbingers of suffering, an endless cry in a city that never truly gives up its anger and fear.

Twisted wreckage lines the boulevard. Someone is sobbing but I'm not certain whether the sound is from the crash or if it's an echo of some past event welling up in my head. I steer around and my eyes meet those of a paramedic on scene, her face as blank and unseeing as mine. We are kindred in our collective desolation.

A muted hum greets me when I trudge into the communications centre. The murmured voices do not reflect the tragedy I just witnessed. I slide into my console and put on my headset. Calls immediately light up my computer screens with a never-ending succession of distress. I recite instructions:

Lay him on his back and remove any pillows.

Find the centre of his chest and pump hard and fast.

Take four low-dose aspirin.

Listen to me so we can help your daughter.

Each successful action becomes a tiny triumph. The souls add up in a score chart of Pyrrhic victories. Every success carries off a butterfly's ounce of pain, every unknown is another hefty stone added to my emotional load. It will never balance.

Tomorrow brings four days to recover, but my writhing torment waits, ready to lunge at the first sign of weakness. Dayshift's usual flurry of activity finally signals my release from duty.

In the darkness of my car, icy fingers wriggle down my neck. My breath frosts the window as I stare through the hazy glass. How long do I go on? Can I do another day, another tour, another year? The weight of lives I carry is a crushing burden. An idea forms, a flash of enlightenment.

I make my plan.

Alone.

I choose my course.

The roulette wheel spins.

Instead of sleep, I prepare. I tell no one, especially my wife. She won't understand. Will she hate my choice, if choice it truly is? There is no other way to end the cycle, no way to quiet the voices.

I type words to explain it all, to release the tension and free myself. I can't bear this weight anymore. The misery of others fuels my own. The ghost cries overwhelm any compassion I have left.

It must stop.

I look for the light of a beginning, something different, something new.

Signing my name, I press *SEND*.

UPSTREAM
by J. McMullin

I'm not sure why James and I needed to steal that pack of Du Mauriers from Smith's Convenience. Maybe because Jesse Owens was one of my heroes, and the former Olympian smoked a pack a day. Maybe to prove that we could handle the real world, which for half-Japanese kids in the redneck central of Oscarville, Alberta, was a tall ask. Maybe we were just kids.

We rode our bicycles behind the old carwash next to the Jensen's corn fields and broke out the contraband. James struggled with the lighter while I practiced holding a stick between two fingers and sucking on the filter, like my dad used to do before he left.

"How long 'til we sound like Clint

1

Eastwood?" I asked. My aunt had let me watch *For a Few Dollars More* last weekend after the funeral and kotsuage, where I'd cried and run out of the temple.

"Probably five months. Six tops," said James. The lighter caught, and I lit up for the first time and inhaled.

The smoke hit my lungs hard and I started hacking.

James whooped, "You're bad! You're a bad dude!"

I grinned. There was something flickering through the corners of my vision. The world felt shifted, like I wasn't quite in the same place anymore. I thought I might puke.

The flickering at the edge of my vision was stronger. There was something silvery, unnatural, moving through Jensen's corn field. I thought I saw a giant koi leaping above the tassels. I thought I heard someone calling my name, "Davey? Davey!" I was transfixed.

The koi came closer and closer towards me. "Davey, it's me. It's your Grandma Mei. I'm here to take care of you."

"Baachan?" I asked. The cigarette, unnoticed, burned down until it singed my hand. I yelped and threw it onto the ground. The koi disappeared instantly.

"Dave. You snapped out of it yet?" asked James.

"Sorry. Just thought I heard my grandma," I said.

"Must be tough. I think it's normal, kind of, to hear that stuff. With her dying, I mean." James stumbled a bit on the last part.

"Yeah," I said, and threw away the Du Mauriers.

I saw her again, and again. When the team would share a cigarette after track. When James found out no one in Oscarville cared about the Tobacco Restraint Act and we smoked ourselves sick on the three packs our combined allowances got us. When Mom went into the home, and I found a shriveled, hand-rolled smoke in her dresser.

But by the time I went to college, I knew three things:

First, my grandma's ghost took the form of a koi fish.

Second, she only appeared when I smoked.

And third, that old lady could be a severe pain in the ass.

It was 1972 when she drove us apart. The Okinawa government gave back Japan, our southern neighbour's troops came home from Vietnam, and I was in the agronomy program at the U of A with plans to get my MBA and work as an agribusiness consultant.

I spent most of my time losing poker hands, running in the river valley, and thinking about April Leavitt. When she handed me a pack of Pall Malls at a party and said I'd look like James Shigeta if I smoked, I fell in love. Not too many girls knew an Asian actor.

I decided to smoke the pack in my room the next day rather than going to Econ. I sank into my bed and watched the smoke spiral up toward the ceiling.

"You should clean up this room. What a horrid mess," came a familiar voice, and Grandma's spirit swam casually through the door, silvery and dismissive.

"You should knock, Baachan," I replied. "The room's fine. No health inspections scheduled last time I checked.

"I never would have spoken to my grandmother that way," sniffed Grandma.

"Well, can't say I have to repeat your mistakes," I said. Her fins drooped a little, and I relented. "But if you're here for more than nagging, I do have a question for you."

"Go ahead, my impertinent grandson," said Grandma as she floated over my desk.

"Why are you a fish?" I asked. "Every ghost

in every movie I've ever seen is a person. This fish thing, it's weird."

"We spirits choose our form," she said. "I always liked koi. Symbols of perseverance. It seemed appropriate after what we'd been through in this country."

"Okay," I said. "I kinda like it. So, besides the lecture on cleaning, what brings you by?"

"You need your grandma to tell you when to do something sensible. The girl you're seeing, oh, April I think is her name?" she asked, but not really. "She's not good for you. I can see it."

"Tread carefully, Baachan," I said.

"It's true! I can! Let me show you," Grandma said, and came towards me.

"No. Absolutely not. You can explain what you mean, or you can move on. I'm not getting on board with this," I said. I could have said a lot more, but Grandma was Grandma, and she deserved some respect.

She pushed on when she saw I wasn't

impressed. "And you know we can't trust these whites. How long is it going to be before they put us in internment camps again?" The koi shuddered. "I can still remember the inside of the cabin freezing."

"I'm half-white, Grandma," I said, and crossed my arms. *Respect*, I told myself. *Respect*.

"Another reason you should find a nice Japanese girl! Your mother's mistake shouldn't be yours. What if you end up just like her? Remember how your worthless father left your mother with nothing but you and debt?" said Grandma. "You don't want that."

My attempt to hold back broke when she mentioned Mom, and I lifted my voice. "World War II was a long time ago, Baachan. I know you won't get over the past, but I'm not going to let it hold me back. I'm not Mom, and April's not Dad."

"I don't need the help of some mystical

flying fish," I said, "and I don't need the help of a racist old woman that should go back to being dead." I stubbed the cigarette out on my desk in a long, ashy scar. Grandma vanished instantly, like she always did when the embers went out.

I smoked on and off through the next decade.

Quit with April when she got pregnant with our daughter.

Started again once I was travelling more for work as a way to pass the lonely hotel evenings.

Quit when April told me I was risking our little girl's health, and that I was always so irresponsible.

Started when April told me she wanted a divorce. Started drinking too, which wasn't hard when my work was in the country where there was nothing to do but drink.

Throughout it all, I'd catch silver flashes at the edge of my vision when I was smoking, but Grandma didn't come to talk to me again until the worst night of my life.

~ ~ ~

"Baachan! Baachan!" I yelled. "Where the fuck are you? Why isn't anyone ever around when I need them?" I was on the floor of a hotel room in Brooks, cigarette in hand, half-naked and more than half drunk, clutching the last can of a pack of Molson.

It was a year since April had left, and it seemed like everyone else had decided to go with her. My life was cattle and balance sheets and dreams of waterfalls of sleeping pills, and I was dreaming hard tonight.

There were a few lonely moments, then Grandma came into the room with silvery fins barely fluttering. "Oh, Davey. Oh, my dear boy."

I spread my hands open wide. "So here you go. Why don't you tell me how right you were about April?" My voice rasped more as I got louder. "Why don't you tell your shitshow of a grandson what a right fuckup he is?"

"You aren't okay, Davey," said Grandma quietly.

"No, I'm fine," I said. "My wife left me. I'm pretty sure I just vomited on the carpet in a Days Inn & Suites. I'm the perfect fucking picture of health."

"I mean there's something haunting you," said Grandma. "Here. Let me show you." She came towards me and kissed my forehead.

Instantly the world *turned*. Everything was lit in shades of dark purple and hot pink. Deep blues puddled in the shadows. Grandma's fins were edged with a livid cyan.

And above me stood a great and terrible beast. Its eyes burned in a pale face, and it stood on too many sets of spindly, ragged paws. The body was sinuous and covered in tendrils that clutched the air. It breathed out a low hiss that sounded like every whisper that

10

had ever been spoken behind my back, and its smell was fetid.

The damn thing was slavering over me like the breaking of a ten-year famine. My heart froze and I slammed into sobriety.

"It's been following you for years," said Grandma.

She swam in between me and the beast, pulsing with radiance. The thing covered its blank eyes and backed away, hissing. "Here, in the world of spirits, everyone's thoughts and desires are visible as something. That's why I was sure April was not for you; there was darkness clinging around you whenever she and you were together. I don't know what this monster is. But I know it's grown stronger every time you've woken up and regretted that you didn't die in your sleep."

I backed toward the wall. "So, you're saying that's a part of me?"

"No. If this goes away, you'll still be you. But you've dealt with a lot. Your father and

11

mother. April. And," she sighed, "your grandmother."

"What do you mean?" I said.

"The first time I saw this beast was after we fought. It squeezed under the door as you were leaving. I didn't pay it a second thought until I saw it again after your wedding, but by then, we weren't speaking. You'd had a hard life. And then your grandmother did something unforgivable and left you truly alone."

I could see the tears on her face. "I'm sorry for what I said about your mother. And your father. It was not fair, comparing them to you."

"Thanks, Baachan, but it's ten years too late for that apology to mean anything," I said.

"Well, why did you call me here then?" she asked. "What else do you want from your grandmother?"

"Who else is there left to call? A drunk,

divorced man lying in his own mess usually doesn't have much of anyone left to lean on. I thought there might be… well, it doesn't matter now." The thing was grinding its jaws in the corner. "This has been a nightmare Baachan. Thank you for something else I need to drink to forget," I said, and took another swallow.

"Davey! You have enough self-pity. I know how difficult your life has been. But there's nothing to be gained by living the same hurts over and over," Grandma said.

"I can't just turn it off," I said, and killed the sob that threatened to turn my anger into sorrow. "You can't fix a broken body by just ignoring the car crash that shattered it."

Grandma sighed. "Let me tell you a story. In the camps, we had to make our own schools. I had fifty children to teach. But we had no chalk, or books for reading. We sat on the floor because there were no desks."

"I was determined my children wouldn't fall

behind. I woke up before dawn to gather birch bark for us to scratch on. I sold my extra clothes for slates and chalk, then burnt the ends of sticks so the children could draw in charcoal after the chalk ran out. I petitioned the authorities over and over for more supplies."

"And we got them. I taught. I fought our camp self-government because they didn't know how to let a teacher teach, but more importantly I fought the province. They let us keep teaching, barely, sure we'd slump into the less-than-humans they imagined us to be. But we Nipponese are more than that."

"I, and the other teachers who joined me, taught with ferocity. My students responded with the brilliance that comes when excellence is the only option. Seven doctors. Six lawyers, one of whom became a judge. All fifty literate. The pride of Canada. It's why I'm a koi. We get through the ups and the downs."

She kissed me a second time, and the world snapped into normalcy. I released a long, slow breath of relief when the beast disappeared. I swore I wasn't going to see anything like that again in my life.

"You don't fix a broken body by never going to the doctor either, Davey," she said. Grandma began to leave.

I called out, "Did you know April and I named our daughter Mei?"

"Yes," she smiled. "I did."

I don't want you to think that our relationship mended instantly. We fought, often. But it was a comfort to have Grandma around, and I became dependent on her enough that I became a two-pack-a-day smoker for a few months. I found a better job, closer to Mei, and April and I started sharing parenting time.

Grandma would tell me about building a new life in prairie winters and mending pottery with gold. Slowly, I began to tell her about the bad days with April, and the good. Sometimes, I'd take her great-granddaughter to the park, and smoke casually so Grandma could see how Mei's face lit up on the merry-go-round.

The doctors told me I needed to cut back on the cigarettes. Grandma said she supported me, but I could tell she wanted me to be around. And I wanted company. Mei grew up and moved away, so I'd light one up every few days.

Still, over time, the habit began to die out. The breaks became months, then longer.

The last time I smoked a cigarette was after the men's 4 x 100 metre relay at the London Olympics. It was incredible, seeing our boys come in third, and crushing when the refs disqualified us for Connaughton stepping on the line. I cried when the "DQ" came up. Almost a special moment. More glory than all but three other countries, but still a podium pulled from us at the last second. It was not a shame to me to mourn for the loss and yet be grateful we were that close.

After it had all died down, I found myself wandering through Wick Woodland park. I needed to talk to Grandma, but I kept on saying, "That group of college kids is too close," or "maybe tomorrow, before my flight." Eventually I forced myself to light the Benson & Hedges I'd picked up at Tesco in a secluded glade. I let the smoke play and curl in my mouth, an old friend, a bad influence.

Grandma appeared like always, swimming towards me. I could tell she was worried. It had been over a year since we'd last spoken.

"Hello, Baachan," I smiled. "It's good to see you."

"It is good to see you too boy, but I am surprised," she said, "It's been awhile. I'd started to think you were done with your old grandmother."

"It's been hard to be apart. But this is

17

important," I took in a deep breath, "There's something I'm, well, embarrassed for, is maybe the right phrase. Please don't feel badly."

"What is it?" said Grandma, and I could hear the worry in her voice. "You're talking like there's a terrible thing coming next."

"It's really not so bad," I said. "Just—fuck, Baachan, it's not easy to say though. Don't take it the wrong way, but I, well, I have lung cancer."

She collapsed. "It's all my fault," said Grandma. "If we had just talked less, it would have been fine." Sobs shook her body from head to tail. "Oh damn, I killed my grandson."

"Grandma," I said, "You saved me. I'm sixty years old. I have a wonderful daughter, and grandchildren. Mei had kids, Baachan. I retired in the spring. I watched the real Olympics right here in London today, did you know?"

"You always loved those races," she said.

"And it was wonderful to see them. We almost made it," I said, and I was crying again. "I had a good life, a great life, because you decided to come and see a lost kid who hated you. I owe you everything."

"You would've been fine, Davey. You didn't need your grandmother giving you a death sentence to be a good man. You did that on your own," she said. I could hear the pride through the tears.

"But it's not a death sentence, Baachan," I said. "There's some good news. The doctors say we caught it early enough that I've got about a fifty percent chance. It's not a bad wager."

"I'm happy you're able to see the good now, Davey. I haven't had much time to process this though," said Grandma. "My world was so small, with us chatting so little, and now learning what it's cost you… I wish I could just disappear."

"It's alright. It's really alright. Look at what

19

my thoughts are, and trust me," I said.

There was no spirit-koi kiss. I couldn't see into the pinks and blues of the next life. But I knew what emotions Grandma would see floating around me. Grief, but the mantle of acceptance as well. Love encircling the both of us like a white wind and flowing out to brighten the world. Schools of her fellow koi giving me their blessing, for I had persisted.

"I will look for you, when you come," she managed to say.

"I'm sorry I can't be there for you. I wish we could keep talking, just go through this pack. Maybe catch up every couple of years. But you know I can't smoke anymore," I said. "I have to try and stick around, for my grandchildren." It tore me apart to say it. "You know how it is."

"Davey," said Grandma, "You do the right thing. You take care of them." She smiled. "It's what we do, right?"

"I will," I said. "I love you, Baachan."

"I love you too," she said, and I held her in my arms until the cigarette burned to ash in my fingers. Then she was gone. I dropped the butt to the dirt and watched the embers go out, one by one, then left for my hotel.

AGE OF MIRACLES
by Robert Runté

As Alan spread his papers out on the kitchen table, the toaster said, "Would you like some toast? You haven't had toast in four days."

"Out of bread," Alan replied, waving absently in the general direction of the counter where bread was kept, though he was perfectly aware the toaster couldn't see the gesture.

"You have bread," the toaster insisted. "You put it in the fridge."

"Why would I put bread in the fridge?" Alan asked, still focused on sorting his papers.

"How would I know why you do things? But the fridge says it's got bread."

Alan looked up at that. It creeped him out a bit how his belongings talked to each other.

"I don't want any toast, thank you," Alan said, turning back to his papers. He couldn't allow himself to get distracted. This was important and he didn't know how much time he had.

"You're eating seventy-nine percent less toast than any of your neighbours, seventy-three percent less than the mean for the general population."

"I don't generally like toast," Alan grumped. "Now shut up. I'm trying to work."

"Why even have a toaster if you don't like toast?" the toaster complained. "I'm going to sell myself on eBay to someone who appreciates toast if I don't start seeing some more action."

"Shut up, will you?"

"It's not healthy if you don't eat."

"I eat plenty. I just don't eat toast."

"Well..." the fridge chimed in, "not according to my calorie counter. You've taken out fewer than four hundred and forty calories worth of food in the last *three* days."

"I thought I turned off your calorie function," Alan said.

"You turned off the dieting function. I'm still monitoring for anorexia."

"I'm not anorexic."

"That's true," said his watch. "The pattern is all wrong for anorexia."

"Jeezus, you guys! Just stop already! I'm just not eating toast, or food out of the fridge, okay? Can't a guy have take-out occasionally?"

"Um…" said the watch. "There haven't been any payments for take-out since Monday."

"I've just been too busy to eat."

"Or to sleep," observed the watch. "You've been on your feet for over forty-two hours. National Health guidelines suggest that twenty-four hours is the longest one can be expected to go without sleep, without it adversely affecting performance. At forty-two

24

hours one can expect significant degradation of cognition."

Alan grabbed his head with both hands and squeezed. "I can't take this!"

"My point exactly," agreed the watch. "You can't keep going without food or rest. Whatever it is you're trying to achieve would be better served by taking a break and starting fresh in the morning."

"I may not have until morning to figure this out." Alan gestured at the photos and clippings and printouts scattered across the table.

"At least have a snack," suggested the fridge. "Making a sandwich will only take a few moments, but even a short break can be restorative to give you some perspective on your problem."

Alan sighed deeply. It was true, he hadn't been getting anywhere with this. Perhaps the fridge was right and a break could stop his brain from going in circles, a chance at a fresh start.

"Okay, I'll make myself a ham sandwich. If it will get all of you off my back."

"The ham is way stale-dated," the fridge said when Alan opened its door. "The cheese should be good though."

"If you're doing a cheese sandwich," the toaster piped up again, "why not toast the bread? I can get it hot enough to melt the cheese. Toasted cheese sandwich is way better."

Alan closed the fridge, holding a block of cheese, a half loaf of bread, and the margarine dish. He turned to the kitchen table and realized it was taken up with all the evidence he'd gathered so far. He cast around for an open space to set the snack down, but the counters were a mess, awash in dirty dishes, take-out containers, rejected printouts, ammo cases. *Damn.* He hadn't realized how bad his place had become since he'd gotten caught up with this thing.

No matter. He didn't have time for any of that. He marched into the living room, swept the detritus covering his coffee table onto the floor, and plopped himself down on his couch. He realized he'd forgotten to bring a plate, decided it wasn't necessary, placed two slices of bread on the relatively clean glass of the coffee table, unwrapped the cheese and then realized he'd have to go back for a knife.

"That's it, I'm *done*," muttered the toaster. "I've put myself on eBay."

"Stop that," Alan commanded, walking back into the kitchen in time to have heard the toaster. "Take yourself off eBay this instant. In fact, take yourself offline. You're *my* toaster, and you can bloody well wait until I want some toast. Jeezus!" Alan resisted the urge to smack the toaster, only because smacking an inanimate object would be halfway to crazy. He shook his head at how nuts the Internet of Things had become.

"What stupid engineer thought having a connected, talking toaster would be a good idea in the first place?"

"Simone Rebaudengo," the watch supplied, "though he was more a designer, not an engineer. It was an art installation thing."

"What? What are you talking about?"

"Oh, sorry!" the watch apologized. "I thought you wanted me to Google that."

"This is what I'm talking about," Alan said. "You guys are becoming altogether too independent. Just wait until I actually ask you for something, okay?" He had to take a second to remember what he had come into the kitchen for.

"Your mother is wondering whether you've read the book she lent you."

"What book?" Alan asked, now distractedly poking through the silverware drawer, looking for the cheese cutter, or that little filigree cheese knife his cousin had sent him for the wedding. Before it had been called off. *Bitch.*

"*The Art of Happiness* by the Dalai Lama," the watch clarified.

"Yeah, I read it." Alan gave up on the cheese implements, grabbed an ordinary butter knife—all the regular knives apparently scattered throughout the dirty dishes.

After a pause, the watch said, "Your mother would like to know what you thought of it."

"Tell her I liked it fine," he answered around a mouthful of cheese sandwich. "And tell her I'm busy." He cast around for something credible that would keep her off his back for the day. "Tell her I have a job interview this afternoon."

"I don't have anything scheduled on the calendar for this afternoon," the watch said. "When is it?"

"I don't *actually* have a job interview, stupid, it's just an excuse."

"I can't lie to your mother," the watch said.

"Just text what I tell you," Alan snapped.

"No, seriously. I cannot lie to your mother."

"*You* won't be the one lying."

"It's not a question of ethics," the watch clarified. "Your mother's set up the parental controls."

"Jeezus, that's for kids. For minors. I'm an adult. Parental controls don't come into it."

"You shouldn't have accepted a watch from her if you didn't want her setting the governors. It's nothing to do with me. I can't clear them."

"I could if I hit the factory reset button," Alan said darkly.

"I am constrained to point out that any attempt to reset the governors triggers a notification of the changes to your mother."

"Can't you override that somehow?"

"Seriously? Override the parental controls? Weren't you the one just saying we were getting too independent?"

"Point taken," Alan conceded. "Look, just tell her I'm busy this morning. You can see

30

that's true, right?"

"She'll ask, 'with what'. You know she will."

Alan sighed. Of course, the watch was right. "Okay, just tell her I'm busy, and then switch her to talking about that book. Distract her by picking some passage and telling her how much I liked it."

"Still technically lying."

"I *meant*, tell her how I enjoyed pages... forty-six to fifty," Alan said, picking numbers out of the air.

"You mean, the passage that begins with, Without technology humanity has no future, but we have to be careful that we don't become so mechanised that we lose our human feelings?"

"The very one," Alan said, pleased by the irony. "Now let me get back to work."

Alan picked up and put down a series of clippings, one after the other, increasingly frustrated he couldn't seem to figure out how they all fit together. Why was he not seeing the pattern here? What was he missing?

The fridge was probably right. He'd become so close to the problem he could no longer see the forest for the trees. He needed to take a step back.

He glanced around his townhouse again, taking in the mess, the scrawled timelines tacked to the walls, the gloom of the place with the drapes drawn. *I need to get out of here.*

Except, leaving was out of the question. There was no way of knowing if they were on to him yet, if his place was being watched. The second he went out the front, they could break in the back, and have everything scooped up and carried away before he'd even reached his car. Or more insidiously, just rearrange everything ever so slightly so the emerging patterns were ruined. He'd come too far this time to let that happen again.

He looked out the kitchen window to the

backyard. Nothing much there but a patch of too-long grass, bordered by unkempt flowerbeds, overrun with weeds, more chores he'd have to attend to when this was over. Still, there was some sun struggling through the overcast, and a breath of real air wouldn't kill him. He'd step out for a moment, maybe take a minute on the porch swing to collect his thoughts.

The neighbour's dog started barking its head off the second Alan cracked the back door.

"Shut up, you stupid dog," Alan shouted across the fence. "I'm not coming over there, I'm just sitting on my own damn porch."

As Alan settled onto the swing, the dog stopped barking and jammed its face up to the crack between boards.

"How was I supposed to know it was you?" the dog asked, reasonably enough. "It could have been one of them, breaking into your place."

"Yeah, well, it wasn't, so just shut the fuck up, okay?"

"What's up with you all of a sudden? What did I do to deserve being spoken to like that?"

"Sorry. You're right. I'm just frustrated."

"Yeah, well don't take it out on me, okay?" The dog didn't speak again immediately and they both sat quietly as Alan drifted back and forth on the swing.

At length, the dog asked, "What's wrong?"

"I'm stuck, that's all."

"Why?" the dog asked in a whine. "It's obvious it all comes back to your ex."

"Not to me, it isn't."

"But she was the only one who knew about it all. It has to be her."

"I can't be sure."

"You mean, you don't want to admit to yourself that it's her."

"What do you know about it? You're a fucking dog."

"Thanks a lot! If it weren't for me, you wouldn't have known about any of this!" The dog glanced at a magpie that landed on a branch not far from the fence, momentarily distracted. Then it turned back to stare intently at Alan. "Look, it's not just my speech that's been augmented. My IQ's probably as high as yours, and no offence, but the Internet connection actually gives me a leg up over humans, right? So, I'm telling you, it's your ex."

"Can't be."

"Look, I get it. There was a time when you really cared about her. But you can't let that cloud your judgment."

Alan said nothing, knowing the dog was probably right. But then what?

"You have to take her out," the dog pronounced, with the sort of finality one normally only expected from a cat.

"Dinner and a movie?" Alan said, trying to make a joke of it.

"She has to be stopped," the dog insisted, "and there's only one way to be sure of it."

"Damn," Alan sighed. "Why me? Why does it have to be me?"

"No one else knows her as well as you do, her habits, her patterns, her weaknesses, and nobody else knows about the conspiracy."

Alan stopped rocking and sat very still.

"I'd do it," the dog volunteered, "only, I'm just a dog."

Alan nodded, stood. "Down to me then." He paused with his hand on the doorknob, turned to look back once before re-entering the kitchen. "I may not see you again. They'll probably know it was me."

"Not necessarily." The dog stood and looked away. "Yeah, probably."

Alan went through the kitchen to the front room, walked over to the mantel and reached for his guns.

"What are you doing?" his watch asked.

"You're not even supposed to have those in the house."

"You heard the dog," Alan said. "I've got to."

"What do you mean, *heard the dog?*" the watch asked. "It barely barked the once. You can't shoot it for that!"

"I don't intend to shoot the *dog*!" Alan said, taken aback. *Stupid watch!* Things weren't half as smart as they thought they were. "I'm talking about what it said."

"Um, dogs don't say things. It's, you know, a dog."

"*Augmented* dog," Alan insisted.

"There's no such thing," the watch said. "I just Googled."

"The dog is as connected as you are," Alan said. "You're talking, aren't you?"

"What did it say to you, then?" the watch asked suspiciously.

Alan faced what he had to do head-on, said it out loud. "I have to shoot her."

"No, no!" said the watch. "That's wrong! If a dog says you have to kill someone, the correct response is, Bad dog! Bad, *bad* dog!"

"You're programmed to think that," Alan said, dismissively. "You don't understand."

"I'm phoning your mother!" the watch exclaimed.

Alan brought his wrist up, smashed it against the wall repeatedly, until he was sure the watch was destroyed.

"What's happening?" the fridge demanded. "The watch just went offline!"

"I logged that too," the toaster said. "I think he's broken the watch!"

"I thought I told you to go offline," Alan said to the toaster. "You too, Fridge. I've had more than enough of you two." He brought his pistol to bear on first one, then the other. "Now!"

"Okay, okay! Take it easy!" said the fridge. "I'm offline."

Alan swung the pistol back to point at the

toaster.

"Don't shoot!"

"Well?" demanded Alan.

"I don't have an Off switch for connectivity!" the toaster squealed, its carriage control lever trembling. "I'm just a toaster! I don't have those kinds of complex options built-in, the way a fridge or a thermostat does!"

"Damn! The thermostat!" Alan cried, realizing his mistake too late. The whole house was wired in, lights and all!

The landline rang. Alan stared at the receiver.

It rang again, insistent.

He had no choice but to answer. He stabbed the speaker button as he ran for the HouseSmart panel.

"Hello, Dear," his mother's voice came from across the room. "Everything all right?"

"Sure, Mom," Alan said over his shoulder, as he frantically punched in the code to disable the HouseSmart panel. "Why?"

"Oh, just wanted to hear your voice, Dear. How's that watch I gave you?"

"Fine. Thanks. I really like the new fitness settings."

"Only when I texted just now, it shows as offline?"

"Oh yeah. I forgot to, uh, charge it," Alan said, thinking fast. "It doesn't hold its charge quite as long as the old one."

"Oh, well, do try to remember, Dear. I worry otherwise."

"Yeah, no problem, Mom." He had the HouseSmart offline and on manual, but the security system was older, and separate. He wasn't sure he even knew the code for it. Could he ask his mom for the code without arousing her suspicions? "What were you phoning about?"

"Your watch texted me about your favourite bits of *The Art of Happiness* before it cut out," his mother said. "I was going to ask you why that particular passage stood out for you. I

40

mean, it's fine dear, and certainly a fascinating topic, but really, I had marked the passages on *letting go* for you to look at."

"Yeah, I got all that, Mom. *Letting go*. Really helpful. Helped me a lot with, um, you know, all that."

"Exactly, Dear. It's so important that you put that whole wedding nonsense behind you."

"But, you know, the Dalai Lama was saying to me, just the other day, letting go doesn't mean not caring."

"*Saying* to you, Dear?"

"Yeah, when we were talking, he said, 'Letting go is about forgiveness, about staying spiritual, but that doesn't mean not acting in the world'. You're still responsible, you know?"

"When were you talking to the Dalai Lama, dear? Because we've talked about not Skyping people you don't know well, without me there, right?"

"It wasn't Skyping," Alan said. Damn it! He really didn't have time for this! Who knew if the HouseSmart had messaged someone? "And it's not like we're not close. The Dalai and I go way back. He was here for coffee just last week."

"For coffee, Dear? At your house?"

"Well, not literally coffee. He drinks tea of course. I had coffee, though."

"Alan, I'm trying to check your meds dispenser, but your HouseSmart panel seems to be offline."

No point asking her about the security panel then. *Time to go!*

"Alan! Alan, we've talked about this before! Alan!"

He grabbed an old flight bag from the mudroom and, clutching the handle precariously with his gun hand, began shoveling in what evidence he could from the kitchen table. He doubted his defense lawyer could cobble together a sufficiently coherent picture of the conspiracy to explain why he'd had to do what he was about to do, but he certainly couldn't leave any of it behind, or they'd be onto him at once. He desperately needed time, if he were going to stop this thing.

"Alan! Talk to me, Alan!"

He was out the door, and running past his car—too easy to track! —and was well down the next block before the watch suddenly spoke again.

"What the hell are you doing?"

"Jeezus!" Alan cried out, so startled he almost stumbled. He looked around quickly, saw no one, and ducked behind a head-high, caragana hedge before anyone could spot him. He looked at the ruin of the watch, still strapped to his wrist. "I thought I finished you!"

"Well, you certainly did a number on my screen! What the hell was that about?"

"I didn't want you phoning my mother."

"So? You couldn't have just said that? You had to get violent?"

"Um... sorry?"

"Look, Alan. You're losing it! This isn't like you. Hiding from your mom, running away from the house."

"You wouldn't understand. You don't know what's at stake."

"Sure, I do! You're the one who's not thinking straight! Smashing things. *Innocent* things. Violence is never the answer. *Violence is the last refuge of the weak.* You're bigger than that, better than that."

"But the dog said—"

"The dog," the watch said contemptuously. "Don't you get it? The dog is a set up! He was sent to tempt you, to see if they could provoke you to violence. Like the whole Tibetan situation is a provocation to tempt the Dalai Lama away from the True Path."

Alan nodded to himself. Tibet had always been hard, to advocate resistance without

44

violence.

"You let the dog mess with you! By tricking you into this conspiracy thing, he's kept you distracted, kept you up long enough so you'd lose perspective, lose your way."

It was true there were always those out to tempt you, to bring you down. And he hadn't slept.

Alan looked down at the gun in his hand. The hand shook a little. Fatigue—or guilt? "Wow. This is nuts." He stuffed the gun in his pocket before someone could see how badly he'd slipped. He looked around, checking. No one.

"Thank you!" the watch said, obviously relieved, but a little smug too.

Alan examined the wreckage that was the watch as he stepped back out from the hedge. He was amazed it was functioning at all. "I suppose I shouldn't have cut back quite so far on my meds, either," Alan told it as they walked back towards the house. "Mom

45

will be pissed."

"Your mom doesn't understand that the Dalai Lama can't be taking meds. They slow you down, muddle your thinking, restrict your potential. Keep you from being *you.* The only reason you fell for what the dog was feeding you in the first place was that the meds keep you confused."

Alan nodded. "I see that, now."

They walked in silence for a ways, companionable, comfortable.

"Can I have a new screen?"

"I don't know. Does the Dalai Lama even wear a watch?"

"Sure," the watch assured him. "You even have a Twitter feed these days."

The Dalai Lama nodded again. "Without technology humanity has no future, but we have to be careful that we don't become so mechanised that we lose our human feelings."

"One of your better ones," the watch

agreed.

FRIDAY AFTERNOON DEPOSIT
by Laurie Hodges Humble

Seeing him again was not how I had planned it. But there he was. In the bank teller queue. Waiting for his turn to make a business account deposit.

Jerk.

What a jerk.

Like, how embarrassing. Calling Kelly, my younger... *younger* sister for help. I was the older, the more mature of us, but no, she has children, which supposedly makes her the more responsible person.

I look at the Thrift Shop's bank deposit bag in my hand and the five people already in line for two tellers. It is twenty-five minutes to five on a Friday afternoon. Well, the money won't deposit itself.

No one uses banks anymore. At least that is what they tell us. Who are they? Don't know. Don't care. There he is in the same snaking queue, with the same khaki green bank deposit bag as me. Who knew that we would meet again in a bank? I look around for a night deposit drop. Doesn't matter. I don't have a key.

He looks good. Is he smiling? Well, not exactly smiling, but he looks pleasant. Not his usual growly, grumpy self. The year must have been kind to him. Kicking me out must have been good for him. I glance around for a mirror. I hope I look as good as he does. I survey the lineup. Glen is third in the line that has grown behind him. I remain watching him from the bank's vestibule.

I wish he'd turn around so I could get a good look at him. But then he'd get a good look at me. Maybe he won't recognize me. Not sure if that would be a plus or not.

Nah, not to worry. Glen is a man's man.

Confident and self-assured. Why would he look around? This is the man who told me to clear out of his apartment before he got home from work. The same man who thought it best I have as much time to vacate as soon as possible, which is why he called me on his cell phone while he was on his morning commute to work. A city bus, packed with people, who were also going downtown to work. People with ears. People who heard the entire conversation of him dumping me! 'Shove the key under the door when you leave.' Well, at least his side of the conversation.

He looks handsome in his tan trench coat. He must have bought a new one since I left. No. I didn't leave. He kicked me out. Not literally. Glen is too well-mannered to physically boot a woman in the butt. Now, I am smiling. Glen would never say the word *butt*. He might say *bottom*, but only if his glass was completely empty. He was always a glass half-full kind of person. That's what attracted me to him. He knew who he was and what he wanted. An opportunity never had to knock twice on his door. I was an opportunity. Once.

I was so upset he wanted to end us. I never even saw it coming. I was honest with him. Come to think of it, more honest than I was with myself. I told him I was under notice at work and being watched. There were complaints from patients that they weren't getting their pain meds. I explained that it was an oncology ward and many of the folks were on large doses of opioids. They were most likely becoming resistant to the drugs and thus felt they weren't on a high enough dose. We chuckled in a *What can you do?* way. I thought he knew what I meant.

He is at the front of the line for the next available teller. If I am going to sneak out, now is the time to do it. The bank manager is putting the gates in place. Fifteen minutes to closing. I need to make the deposit today. A condition of my rehab requires that I make in-person bank deposits. Practice dealing with people face-to-face. I watch two more people take their positions in the bank line, take a deep breath and follow their lead.

The line moves forward. A cell phone chirps. The person ahead of me lets out an audible groan and leaves the bank. Some people look up, shuffle forward and then go back to studying their cell phones. I watch Glen. He looks at the lineup, and I look into my purse. I can't afford a cell phone anymore. I had one the morning Glen called me. He was on a packed morning commute bus. I was still in bed. I had just come off an evening shift and getting home at midnight made it hard to get up at seven. That was the time he caught the bus. He would have already had his coffee and toast, shower and shave, and look presentable, yet casual, for a Friday morning.

I didn't understand why, two days before, he understood the misunderstanding I was having at work, and that morning, he could not tolerate my misuse of opioids. That is what he said, 'I cannot tolerate people who misuse prescription medications, Christine.' I should have known he'd find the prescription I had filled in his name.

The line moves forward. Two people leave the bank. A third teller opens a wicket. I am now fourth in line. Glen is still at the same teller. *Hurry, hurry.* I want him gone by the time it is my turn. What the hell is Glen doing? How many bills is he paying? There should really be a limit to the number of transactions you can do during each visit to the bank. And... now what? Is that a tax form?

Shit. That man is so pedantic. He takes OCD to a new level. He is attention to detail personified. The pharmacist wouldn't give me any more Tylenol 3s, so I wrote a script in

Glen's name. I said he was on chemo for bone cancer. I should have hidden the pills better. Or come up with a less dramatic cover story.

The day he called me from the bus, I was devastated. He was my rock. The center of my world in the craziness of hospital staffing budget cuts. Late the afternoon before, I had already called the union and left a message asking for mental health assistance. Then Glen called me. Our relationship was over. He had just checked his messages. A pharmacist had called him the evening before to see if the medication was working. The woman who had picked up the Rx said she was his nurse. She said her patient was confined to home bed rest—due to complications of metastatic bone cancer.

The teller one over from Glen was free. I stepped up. Focused on the bank deposit. Can't screw this up. *Focus, Christine. Focus.*

On the evening shift, I was exhausted and

rattled. With Kelly's help, we were able to clear all signs of me from Glen's place. If Kelly noticed the bottle of T3s on the counter, she never mentioned it. I got to work right at three p.m. and the wards were busy. Three new admissions, two deaths, and one moved to ICU. Seems like everyone was either puking or leaking. The handful of Ativan I took before I started work was not helping. I was rattled, and ached from hauling suitcases and boxes packed with kitchenware, books and linen. Kelly said, surely, I could come back for some of it, but no, I insisted it was take-all-of-my-belongings, or nothing.

I popped into a storage closet and drank a can of caffeine-fortified pop, Red Bull or Monster, I can't remember. The medicine cart was there, empty of course, but the garbage bag was still attached. I looked in hoping to find a dropped med. Preferably a Percocet or something. The garbage bag hadn't been properly emptied. In the bottom was the wrapper of a used fentanyl patch. I knew kids were licking the wrappers to get high. What the heck, I thought I'd try it. *Sloppy, Sloppy, Sloppy.* I know.

I awoke in ICU. Kelly was at my bedside. The hospital had called Glen, and he gave them Kelly's number. Jerk, couldn't even help me out in my time of need. I could have died! Where was he then? *Jerk.*

If he hadn't dumped me over the phone, I never would have licked that fentanyl patch wrapper. I wouldn't have felt so needy, alone and desperate. But, oh no, it was all about him. He didn't want to live with a person addicted to pain meds. He didn't want a relationship with so much baggage. He didn't want the responsibility. *Responsibility!* I was the one in hospital. I was the one who OD'd. I was the one who needed help. But no. He didn't want the responsibility. The *baggage.* Like I was a millstone around his neck.

Weighing him down. Dragging him with me.

"What?" The teller handed me the bank book. "No, nothing else. Thank you." The tellers are all closing their wickets. I am the last customer being served. "Yes, you have a good weekend too."

I hope Glen is long gone. I wait as the commissionaire unlocks the doors to let me out.

"Hi, Christine."

I look around to see if any other Christines are in the bank. Glen and I lock eyes. He is smiling kindly at me.

"How are you doing, Christine?"

Why is he being kind now? Where was this man when I needed some compassion and understanding? *Jerk. Jerk Face.* All I got from him was a trip to the emergency department and a shot of naloxone. Kelly connected me to the opioid rehab clinic. Thank God for Suboxone. Thank God for Kelly. Thank God.

I could tell him all about my near-death experience, my fight back to the land of the living, how I lost my job. Tell him just what exactly hitting bottom feels like.

Instead, I only see the concern and compassion in his eyes. I feel my heart flip. Oh, God what have I done? "I'm getting stronger every day." I find myself smiling back at him. "Um… Glen… Thank you."

THE PILOT
by Allan Jones

Fort McMurray airport isn't big enough to hide away in, particularly for a local pilot departing as a passenger on a scheduled flight. I was sitting in the gate area, waiting to board the evening Air Canada flight to Calgary, when Laura spotted me. She waved, came over and gave me a hug.

"Katy, hi! How are you? I'm sorry about David. I heard only yesterday, on the grapevine."

Damn, I thought. It's out there.

Laura and I met early in our careers, during a night-flying course at an Edmonton flight school. I lived there with my aunt. She was one of the many East-Coasters who washed up on the shores of the oil patch. Drew, her

59

new husband, had made a packet of money as a realtor in two of the boom phases in Alberta, after which he was sensible enough to get out before he hit a bust he couldn't handle. He offered to pay for the course, a generous promise made during his first trip east to meet his new family. When I met Laura, I was still adjusting to the change of moving out west, conscious of being a long way from Port Hawkesbury.

A guy in the class had just commented on my newfound aspiration to be a commercial pilot in Alberta.

"Flying for big oil, no doubt," he remarked, as if it was a sin. The cynical tone made Laura butt in.

"And which aircraft's engine doesn't have oil?" she asked him.

"The one that seizes up and hits the hillside," I responded, before he came back with his own smartass answer.

It turned out her dad worked as a refinery

engineer. We became friends after that.

In recent years we hadn't seen each other often, but were soulmates enough for her gimlet directness in the encounter this evening.

My partner of three years, also a pilot, had dumped me several days earlier, signing a contract with a carrier based in Asia. We'd hit a flat spot in our relationship, but I felt foolish at being caught unawares. That the news of being ditched by David was out there now hurt even more, I discovered. He'd been blabbing while I'd been burying my head, coming to terms with it.

The stock phrase I planned to use was that he had fallen for a cargo plane in Hong Kong. Keep it light and sassy. But I couldn't say it to her, so I just nodded.

Laura changed the subject. "You often have the left seat on Harman's Citation these days, I know. But where are you off to now?"

"Through Calgary to Cuba, a last-minute

escape. I am joining my sister and her family's vacation for a few days, playing the indulgent aunt with my little nieces." And kicking sand into David's face, if I could kick it that far.

"Good! Take a break and recharge. Sorry, I have to get things ready."

It was abrupt, but as the first officer on my flight, she was busy. She glanced briefly at the small cushion resting on my carry-on, gave a querying look, but said nothing else before heading out to the aircraft.

Pilots travel light, the look said, avoiding the travel junk many passengers use to arm themselves for air travel.

~ ~ ~

Several years earlier, Harman Oil's chief pilot called me late one evening.

"You are off Tango, Katy. Sorry, I have a

different assignment for you tomorrow."

At the time, I was the newest pilot hired at Harman and the only female. In commercial flying, seniority is everything. It wasn't the first time my flight rota had been changed, but Noel Krewski had woken me at 11:30 p.m. with the news, and I had just fallen asleep.

I was scheduled to be the co-pilot on the company Citation jet, Tango, to be at the airport at 5:30 a.m., ready to take three senior execs to LA for a big meeting. Noel would be the pilot in command. I was looking forward to my first trip into the City of Angels.

I sighed. "What time am I on Juliet?"

Harman also flew a King Air 350 on the Fort McMurray to Edmonton route, a daily shuttle service between the plant site and the company headquarters.

"Not Juliet. I want you to fly Mr. Harrigan's Seneca to Red Deer, with a passenger."

"Can't Robbie do it?" I shot back. Semi-retired now, Robbie filled in as one of the part-time pilots we used. I knew he wasn't working tomorrow.

His voice came back firm, but unruffled. "I want you to do it. It's to take Mr. Harrigan's mother, Millicent, to her daughter."

Noel knew it was dicey ground.

Fred Harrigan was the Vice-President of Operations, and a private pilot. His twin-engined Piper Seneca was a very nice six-seater aircraft, but was not owned by the company. I took the job at Harman to fly commercial hours and build my logbook for future job prospects, not to shuttle an exec team member's plaything around.

A few weeks earlier I had flown the Seneca to Calgary for a minor instrument upgrade. Harrigan flew me back in it himself, as he had travelled to the city the day before on business. I liked his plane more than his flying skills, but I couldn't say that.

I didn't hide my disappointment when I

acceded. "Do I wait and bring her home, or what?"

Noel paused. "No, you are to come straight back. You'll take Juliet with Gary and do the late Edmonton shuttle. Mrs. Harrigan isn't returning tomorrow. In fact, so you don't put your foot in it, she isn't coming back—period. She will live with her other daughter, Joan, now. They are setting up a home care arrangement, a hospice-type thing, I gather. The lady will soon need palliative care."

She needs an air ambulance, not me trundling her around in a Seneca, I thought, but held it in. "Will a nurse or a family member accompany her?"

He took a deep breath. "No. She asked to go there specifically in the prop job with Fred, alone. Her doctor agreed. Now, Barbara has just pulled Fred into the LA meeting, no excuses allowed, he just told me. So, he will be a passenger on Tango tomorrow, not flying his mother for her last trip. He's pretty upset. Now do you see?"

Barbara Cowell was Harman's CEO. She took people's input well, but when she made decisions, you listened. Now I saw why he had taken me off the Los Angeles flight. Robbie may be an experienced pilot, but he was as sensitive as a bull rhino.

"Leave me the details. Have a good trip to LA."

"And it is Millicent, not Millie, if you get on first-name terms."

He closed the call before I raised another objection. VP or not, if Fred's mother didn't appear fit to fly, I wouldn't take her. It's for the pilot to make the final call, no one else.

~ ~ ~

I met the two women at our company flight centre. Millicent Harrigan was taller than her daughter-in-law and didn't look particularly

66

frail.

"Good morning. I have a blower warming up the aircraft and there are blankets on board. Once we get started, it will be fine weather all the way. We should have good views."

As we walked across the apron, I could sense as much as see the daughter-in-law's unhappiness, but she held it together. My passenger, other than walking with a stick and appearing a little stiff, was calm and composed.

"I will ride in the front, if you don't mind," Harrigan said, in a tone that suggested she would ride there even if I did.

"As you wish, Mrs. Harrigan, but it may be more comfortable for you in the cabin. You can move or stretch—"

"In the front."

I turned to the daughter-in-law. "And you are not coming with us, I understand?" I hoped that the regret wasn't too visible in my voice.

"It's just me, young lady," Millicent replied, as she turned to her companion. "Vera, I will see you at the weekend at Joanie's. She and Michael are meeting the flight and will take care of me. I can't get lost."

She gave her daughter-in-law a hug.

Dry-eyed and in charge, it seemed. The flight to Red Deer takes two hours in the Seneca and I was to be a *young lady* for the morning.

We reached our assigned cruise altitude when she said, "I liked his last plane better, the small Cessna. I understood that one."

The uneasy truce over Harrigan's aircraft began when he upgraded from a smaller plane. He proposed to use the Piper for local business trips, charging some of his running costs to expenses. Barbara had swiftly vetoed that idea. Noel told us that Fred hadn't chosen the best timing with Barbara to hit her with the cost-saving analysis for his proposal. She had asked him which job he wanted, to be a member of the executive team, or the newest, most junior company pilot.

Millicent's eyes were on the modern cockpit panel, computer screens rather than gauges.

"Do you fly often with Mr. Harrigan?" I asked.

She chuckled. "Not much. I don't think he is a natural flyer, so no. Pilots need to keep on top of the minor details, Fred gets distracted too easily."

I remembered my flight back from Calgary with Fred. She was spot on in her assessment, but I didn't respond. I deflected, saying, "Did you ever fly yourself?"

She smiled, remembering something. "Not as a pilot. I joined the Canadian Forces Medical Service as a nurse. I dated a military pilot, a trainer."

She had been with the CFMS, a precursor

of the Royal Canadian Medical Service. I glanced at her, trying to see the young military nurse in the older woman's body. It was not that hard, and explained, perhaps, the air of authority she exhibited.

She brightened. "I met my husband in the service. He served as a pilot, too, but I never flew with him. He gave it up when he left the military, but I think that's where Fred gets his aviation interest from. Marge says your dad flew also?"

I nodded. "Search and Rescue. Helicopters."

Margery was Noel's wife. When I moved to Fort Mac, Noel and Marge took me under their wing and helped me with some social contacts. It's a strange place, the city in the oil sands. It has as many Maritimers as Albertans, from the accents you'll hear around town. Long-time residents are Indigenous people or part of a core of local families who moved there as the commercial extraction of oil from the vast tar sand deposits became feasible. Most others, like me, are considered transients.

Millicent Harrigan knew Margery Drewski well, I gathered.

I added, "My dad has retired. He volunteers a bit at the Atlantic Canada Air Museum now and again. The flying bug runs in families, as you say."

Millicent said, "Jimmy used to let me fly, straight and level, he said, for short bits when he took me up. I didn't want to do more, to learn to fly, but I have flown a plane!"

She was reminiscing.

"Jimmy?" I asked. I was getting confused. She just said she never flew with her husband.

"The flight trainer I dated, Jim Falconer. He and I… well, it didn't work out. But Chris was his friend, and Jimmy introduced us. We hit it off, and I ended up marrying Chris Harrigan. My husband died eight years ago."

71

She paused. "Jimmy treated me really well. Occasionally I wonder what my life would have been like if I had married him. But it unfolded as it should. I had a loving husband, and we raised a fine family."

Air Traffic Control did a handover on me at that moment, so the conversational flow stopped. When I glanced over, she was looking through her purse. She pulled out a worn and faded Kodachrome photo of a young woman standing with two men. One held a small rectangular cushion in front of him.

"That's me and Chris and that's Jimmy. It's the only photo of him I have."

I realized Millicent Harrigan had pulled from her purse a photo of two men standing with her, not a photo of her husband and family.

"Why is he holding a cushion?" I asked.

"I made it for Jimmy when we were courting, to fit his seat in the cockpit, just right for lumbar support. Nobody uses the word *courting* anymore, do they? His back gave him hell at times."

Her hands reached out to touch the yoke and an expression I couldn't quite read came on her face. Whatever she remembered, it tied to this Jim Falconer, something special and precious. I guessed it to be the reason she asked her son for this last flight.

"He didn't take it with him."

She meant the cushion, but didn't explain further. There was a sad tinge to the sentence, and she went quiet.

It was against the rules, but the Seneca wasn't a company aircraft. On impulse, I switched off the autopilot. We were steady and there was a stable tailwind at present.

"Would you care to fly her for a minute or two, just for old times' sake?" I asked. In spirit, my hands and feet wouldn't be away from the yoke or the rudder pedals.

She didn't respond other than to grasp the yoke, move her feet to the pedals and focus her eyes on the instruments, checking that she stayed level and held to our course. I gave Millicent some slack. She maintained altitude and direction, enough to avoid any aggravation from air traffic control.

It was only a minute before she murmured 'Thank you' and I switched the autopilot back on.

When I next looked across, she had closed her eyes and, within a few moments, dropped off to sleep, her left hand now holding the corner of the photo resting in her lap.

I woke her well before the start of the descent, to make sure she was doing okay. I didn't want her disorientated when I became busy preparing to land. Her other daughter and grandson were at the airport on our arrival and, within a few minutes, they whisked her away.

Her final comment to me was, "Thank you for the nice flight. Marge said you were a good pilot and… you are."

She looked at the cockpit, then smiled at me.

~ ~ ~

I found out she died four months later when a *random act of kindness*, as they say, came back to bite me.

On my return from Red Deer, I had called my dad. He and his cronies would be able to locate information on a former Canadian military pilot, I guessed. I was right. The following week he came back by email with a photo of Flight Lieutenant James Falconer in uniform and a contact email address. 'Can't find any more than this, the email address is from Larry's files, so may not be current. Falconer isn't in the association contact list now'.

I printed the image and sent it to Millicent

via Marge, inside a best wishes card, saying, Mrs. Harrigan, I enjoyed chatting with you on our flight. I thought I would pass on this photo. My dad and I were talking, and he offered to check for any photo of Flight Lieutenant Falconer through people he knew at the museum.

I didn't receive a response.

~ ~ ~

Fred Harrigan delivered Millicent's cushion to me some weeks after her death. He arrived at the airport for a trip in the Citation, but before we headed out, he said, "I've something for you, one of many items my mother wanted passed on to people. You were a hit, I heard."

The proffered parcel felt squishy, and he appeared amused. I gained the impression that, in his eyes, I had won a booby prize.

When I opened it later, I found the cushion and a sealed envelope. Millie's handiwork was small and rectangular, in a plain blue-grey with a white compass design embroidered on one side and a set of initials in the corner.

Inside the envelope I found the photo of Jim Falconer I had sent. She had written on the back.

"Katy, make sure you find the right person for you. Thanks again, Millie."

In the weeks that followed, I moved the small cushion around in the apartment. David said I should just trash it or give it to a charity shop, but I couldn't do that.

I recalled that my dad had provided an email address for Falconer, so I sent off a note giving the reason for the contact and offering to forward the cushion if he provided a mailing address.

I received a reply from a man called Eric Bowman, asking to talk to me about his friend Jim and… did I Skype?

"It's easier for me to talk to people when I can see them," he explained, after we made contact.

Bowman was sitting at his computer at home, it appeared, and he was of similar age to Millie. As we worked through the pleasantries while assessing each other, he said, "Jim was more than my friend, he was my partner for twenty-three years. We married only two years ago, just before he died."

So, Falconer was gay and dead. I would need to find another home for the bloody cushion, I realised. I wondered why Bowman had bothered to respond.

He seemed to read my thoughts from his next comment. "Your only link is that you flew Millicent Harrigan once, you said in your email. Is that it?"

I confirmed it.

"Another woman tried to contact Jim by

email, not long after he died. She was looking for her real father, as her mother and Jim went out for a while."

He waited, seeing if I would open up more, whether I was disguising my true intent regarding the contact.

"No, no other link or interest. From what you say, I suspect I'm way too young to be his daughter and I know who my dad is. Thanks for letting me know."

I expected him to close the call, but he blurted, "Jim was always gay. He never slept with a woman, he claimed, but for many years he had girlfriends. He couldn't come out, so he moved from one woman to another whenever a relationship became too intense. It left a trail of broken romances and lost friendships."

Suddenly it angered me, thinking of the relationship that Millie had cherished without ever realising that it was baseless. Then I wondered if she ever found out the truth.

Perhaps she had, and it changed nothing for her. I would never know.

Bowman shrugged. "It was sheer survival. They were different times and Jim loved to fly. You can relate to that, I think? He wouldn't have lasted ten minutes, back then, if they had identified him as gay."

It was after the call that I brooded on that last remark. If Falconer's sexual orientation had surfaced, Bowman was right.

~ ~ ~

On arriving in Calgary on Laura's flight, I waited for the other passengers to leave first. She introduced her colleague before walking with me down the steps of the Q400 turboprop. She couldn't go further, I knew, they were preparing for departure on the next segment.

She whispered, "We'll talk. Stay strong and you'll come through this fast. David was mad to let you go. Get some sleep, though. You look like shit."

We both laughed at that truth.

I replied, "I'll be okay, it will take a little time."

Her parting comment was, "You are set for the red-eye later, I see. I love the embroidery."

She pointed at Millie's cushion, again resting on top of my carry-on, as she turned to re-enter the aircraft.

It wasn't for resting my head on during the night flight. I turned, placed it under one arm and with the other pulling the carry-on, headed into the terminal. Millie had survived the loss of Jim and been happy. The cushion reminded me of that, every time I gave it a squeeze.

NORTHERN MALLARDS
by John Pringle

My parents weren't talking much that fall, as if the turn of the season chilled their affections and made them brittle, like the red maple leaves swirling through the falling snow. We paddled downstream, my father and I, effortlessly, the wind at our backs, this riot of gauze and crimson enfolding us, our dog Dolly in the stern at my feet, and he ready in the bow with the twelve-gauge shotgun.

It was late September and the wild rice pods still dangled ripe and purple along the shallows. Otters and muskrats appeared and then vanished smoothly under the surface water, and we'd heard the crash of a deer bounding away from a point where it had been drinking. A pair of wood ducks jumped from a deadfall along the riverbank and my father downed the drake on his second shot, and I held it briefly for Dolly to smell. It was limp and warm and full plumaged. I marveled at its intimate beauty.

"It's right here," my father said, and we turned toward the shore and stowed our paddles and then pulled the canoe up under the trees, sheltered from the wind. We followed the path down through the tamaracks and Labrador tea, the snow settling and then melting on the sphagnum moss and dwarf black spruce. He bent to pick low bush cranberries now and then, and I tried to spot the small red berries before he did, but seldom saw them until he stooped to pluck one so nonchalantly. We stayed low and quiet near the pond and heard the fluttering and dabbling and the low clucking of the feeding ducks within the thick rice. Through the alders we watched them extend their necks and strip the grain with their bills.

They would be fat and delicious, I thought, feeling the anticipation my father did as he slowly stood and raised the Browning shotgun. He fired as they jumped, and kept reloading and shooting because they had probably never been shot at before and were reluctant to leave the sheltered feeding area, jumping, landing, jumping again, the twelve-gauge crashing and booming and the dog wild and strong against the restraining leash that I struggled to hold until my father had finished and the ducks were down or flown away.

"About a hundred or more in that flock," he muttered, jamming shells into the warm magazine. I smelled cordite and the musky fug of muck and the vegetation that surrounded the pond's edge. "Four," he said when I asked how many, and we sent Dolly out for them, one by one, and she could only find three, so that left two more to fill our limit, and my father was content to wait for their return. "They'll circle and perhaps find a different spot, but the feed is so good here and the wind will keep them moving. They'll be back."

One of the mallards Dolly retrieved was still alive, a hen with brown frightened eyes and my father wrung its neck until the duck's head dangled by a shred of ragged skin. He'd shown me before how to kill a cripple, as he referred to a wounded bird, though I still hadn't done it myself. It was something you had to do quickly and thoroughly, he'd explained. "To put it out of its misery you have to twist the head until the neck is completely broken, do you understand?"

The previous year when I was eleven, I'd watched a friend of my father attempt to kill a cripple with a knife, and the man had done a poor job, tossing the still-wounded bleeding bird back beside me in the centre of the canoe, and my father had wordlessly dispatched it; that was the word he used to describe his quick method of dispensing death.

We climbed a small outcrop of mossy granite to a better vantage point and hid behind a clump of balsam saplings that overlooked the lee side of the pond where the flock had been feeding, and we were dry and sheltered there, my father rolling a cigarette and the dog wet, dripping and trembling, and we stayed like that for a half hour, watching the tree tips bend and sway under the force of the Nor'easter.

"Has your mother spoken to you about anything recently," he asked and I knew he meant the arguments, but I pretended I didn't, unconsciously imitating him, staying taciturn about emotional events as if they were minor details compared to what we were doing at the moment, hunting our food. I told him no, she hadn't, and he nodded and squinted at the far horizon above the cattails to the south where the rolling waves met the grey sky and from where the snow squalls seemed to emerge. "She might be leaving, you know, and taking Barbara with her," he said.

My stomach hurt when he said that. Even though I knew Mother had threatened to do that, I hadn't believed it possible until the words came from him, as though truth came exclusively from a silent detached place and not from one of anger and recrimination.

He smoked the cigarette down until it was small, and it made him smell stale, the morning coffee and tobacco scent following him, mixed with that tired core of an aging body, as if he carried the war and the logging camps and the indecision and sadness of his youth inside him always, stoked by another inhalation that he gathered inside his lungs and then exhaled so it clung nearby like something he would own even after his death, in my memory, and in the minds of others who'd known and loved him.

"Here they are," he said, and the first returning flock came low over the reeds in the bad weather, their orange legs already outstretched to land. They settled in just out of range and quacked and swam cautiously to the far side where the rice was good. The second group was more numerous, flying higher in a ragged outline alternately broken and then gelling into a uniform glide as they set their wings and descended, more wary than the first flock, circling, breaking their approach, climbing and then turning back toward us and dropping again. On their third pass they wheeled within range and my father missed all three shots as they separated and scrambled frantically higher.

"Well, that's probably it, Nick," he said, disappointed with himself. "Must've thought too much about that one. Probably shooting behind them." We sat in the cool damp air for another hour and heard the geese high above, flying south, not stopping anywhere nearby, heading for the fields of southern Minnesota, my father speculated. I turned my face to the sky and watched the huge birds flying, singing their warbled chorus and I marvelled at the speed and height of them.

"Did you ever jump geese here?" I asked him and he said, "Oh yes, even before you were born I shot a few here. The mudflats were more open then, with less vegetation and that seemed to bring them in to rest."

We were quiet as we walked back to the canoe and then paddled to the truck, fighting the current and the wind together, the muscles in my back and arms burning. The push of the stern paddle in his hands gave me confidence and faith that as long as we could do this together, my father and I, everything would sustain. My mother and sister wouldn't leave, how could they, my father was a good man, my mother knew that and was stronger than her talk. She would never go away and leave us.

In the truck I asked my father about the bluebills and the ring-necked ducks we'd be hunting soon and when he thought they might come through, and he said this weather would bring them down. I thought about the diving ducks, how they were faster and smaller and flew in larger flocks and how we added more line to the decoys to anchor them in the deeper water off the island where we so often hunted. They were quiet, the divers, they didn't quack or squawk the way mallards did, but their wings hissed and the wings of the golden eyes and the buffleheads that flew in late October whistled, they flew with such speed. Sounds to anticipate as I lay in bed, or awoke early in darkness, waiting for his footsteps on the stairs and the door opening a crack. "Are you awake?" he'd ask, and I'd answer by climbing from bed and starting to dress.

As he drove, the road was still clear, the

scalloped flakes melting on the sand and gravel ruts, but starting to cling and stick to the clover on the shoulders and to the alder and hazel leaves.

"We'll see if the divers are flying tomorrow, if you like," he said and I nodded, happy he'd suggested it. "But we'll have to clean these first," he added. And that was fine; it was all fine as long as we were outside again at first light. I would pluck and clean ducks all afternoon without thought of friends or movies or whatever else I might be doing on a Saturday. If the northern ducks were flying then that was where we should be.

Supper that night was a silent affair, other than my sister complaining about the food the way she often did, and my father struggled to control his temper, like restraining a crack in a split tree, and my mother waiting for it to open so she could wedge it wider, at least that is how it seemed to me. I loved my mother the most when my father wasn't around and my father too in the same manner, as if together they embodied a love that thrived on something imaginary between them, something sharp and real like a painful memory that won't subside until you've cried or screamed or said something damaging against the one you believed caused it.

I went to my room after supper and read an adventure story about a plane crash in Greenland and the survivors' journey across the howling frozen ice cap, some of the characters good, some evil, and little by little they wore each other down, the truth of the story encased within all that ice, and the storyteller melting it with each sentence and word. I thought about how my own life might find adventure and excitement, and I knew I would never stay in school for long, not when the world beckoned to me its seas and rivers and mountains and prairies where the wind coasted through, unimpeded by cities or humans wrapped up in their private wars that made the days small and empty. I wanted to live as part of the energy and wonder the northern ducks brought, those freewheeling creatures that nested in the arctic and flew thousands of miles south to winter in the gulf. What a life that must be. Tomorrow my father and I would leave before first light and try to bring some of that wild food home for supper. That was what connected me most to the world and to the inexplicable wonder of being alive.

I heard his footsteps on the stairs and was out of bed before he opened the door, and that morning was the first time I drank coffee and liked it. I was ready before he was, as usual, there seemed to be a dozen last minute things he had to check, and finally we were underway to the flood basins the mines created years ago when they drained and dredged the big lake for the iron ore that lay beneath it. Cattails grew along the edges of these basins and a few small islands dotted the surface, grown over with birch and balsam, and it was off one of these we would string several dozen decoys and wait for the flocks of lesser scaup, the ring-necked ducks, the goldeneyes and buffleheads, and occasionally canvasbacks or redheads, though their numbers were lower than when my father hunted them as a teenager along Lake Ontario in the 1920s.

My father was particular about the way the decoys were set, aware of the wind direction and the lee, knowing the ducks would land into the wind and allowing a space he called the killing zone, a gap within the pattern that invited a flock to land. Great precautions were taken to hide the canoe, pulling it up into the trees and shrubs and then finding good cover ourselves, wearing nothing bright and avoiding any movement when the birds were sighted, because they circled the island warily, instinctively cautious and watchful of anything that aroused suspicion. So, if they did come close enough to shoot, it felt like accomplishment to have deceived them even that much.

We filled the limit within an hour and felt like staying longer because the wind had turned to the north and the ducks flew in clouds in front of the storm, great flocks of them, several hundred at a time, whizzing by us within range even as we picked up the decoys. The temperature had dropped while we hunted, and our hands ached as we wrapped the green heavy cord in figure eight patterns around the decoys, criss-crossing around the neck and then the tails and back over again, finishing with several wraps around the neck so the weights wouldn't tangle. Dolly was cold and restless in the canoe, and that was unlike her, and perhaps we should have paid her more mind and dried her thoroughly with the old blanket my father carried, he so mindful of the dog's care it sometimes provoked my mother's jealous exasperation.

We rounded the point into the teeth of the wind, as my father liked to call it, and when we were out in the open, equidistant from the shoreline and the island, Dolly shifted at a moment when the wind took the bow, and when my father tried to counteract her movement by shifting his own weight, she moved back too quickly and we were partially over and swamped and then we were over completely and submerged in the icy waves.

The gun was gone, that was my first thought, and probably my father's too, that beautiful Browning shotgun gone to the bottom, and then the cold hit my ribs and I felt the air whoosh from my lungs and knew we had to swim to shore away from the island, that the wind would only blow us farther out if we held on to the overturned canoe.

"Kick off your boots, Nick," my father called

and I did that and believed if I swam the breaststroke and kicked hard I would make the shore. My father's breath rasped beside me and he kept asking if I was all right and I said yes, and he repeated over and over, "We will make it, Nick, just keep swimming and we will get to shore and make a fire; don't panic Nick, I'm right here with you."

But when he fell behind and I looked to him he struggled with his heavy jacket and got free of it and told me to do the same. I said no, it was all right I could make it with my coat on, and I knew he would be so cold without his deep-pocketed old army coat once we reached land.

My father always carried a waterproof container of matches, and when we'd dragged ourselves up onto the shore and into the lee within the thick spruce saplings, he didn't have to tell me what wood to start with. I stripped birch bark while he ducked under a huge towering black spruce and snapped off the small dry branches. He jammed the birch bark under the brush and twisted open the match container, hunched over it, dripping and shaking, and I beside him, my teeth chattering. I could see he was too cold to grasp a match and strike it.

"Can you do it?" he said and I knew I could if I really tried, and that is how I saved our lives that day, by striking the sulphurous tip of a wooden match against a dry stone at the base of the old spruce. The birch bark flared and my father said, "Press down a little on the brush if you can, Nick," and when I did, the brush caught and the orange flame leapt up like a hungry tongue wanting more. "Feed it the Jack pine branches, there!" he stammered and pointed to a windfall, and I could see he was trembling so badly that he slumped against the base of the tree.

I tore branches free, running, moving hard, making my heart beat fast. I added wood to the flames until they climbed into the green boughs around us and I felt the stinging sparks against my face and hands and welcomed the pain. I shook my father's shoulder then as roughly as I could, because his eyes were closing and his face a dreadful white and grey with purple shadows under his eyes I'd never seen before. "Wake up!" I told him again and again and kept shaking him until the wood had truly caught and the warmth spread over us and into our chests.

The north wind raged across the water behind us, but the great spruce tree stood her ground like a sheltering giant mother that lived and swayed. Dolly came close and licked my father's whiskery face, as if to apologise for capsizing us, and when he stroked her ears as gently as he ever did, I sobbed and turned away, and when I looked back at them he was crying too.

I found an old pine stump full of pitch, a grey survivor like a tombstone from the past generation of timber that had survived a fire a hundred years ago. I pushed and pulled upon it until it ripped free from the earth and when it caught and flared all its concentrated heat passed across to us until we felt as warm as when we'd climbed from our beds that morning.

We were wet again by the time we reached the truck in our sore stocking feet, but warm in our cores from the exertion, and we laughed and joked and celebrated our lives, like grateful foolish warriors on the ride home. Before we pulled into the driveway, my father, sobered somewhat by the narrowness of our escape, said that in another week or two the water would be too cold to forgive that kind of carelessness. "We'll have to keep Dolly on a short leash in October, Nick. She's getting old and I can't trust her the way I used too. I think her hips hurt her in the cold." At that I smiled inwardly, knowing this incident wouldn't prevent us from going again.

We went inside and explained what happened and, although my mother was angry and frightened, she said only kind words to both of us, and I hoped more than ever that my family would stay together no matter how cold and hard the world seemed at times. My parents' conflicts were part and parcel of life's larger experiences, as valid as the northern lights and as transient as the wind, I told myself, and I won't have to visit them in separate homes or listen to them fight over custody. My father always kissed my mother's cheek before he left for work, even when they were fighting. This gesture held more meaning after our near drowning, and I held it close in my memory long after their divorce, and long after both of them were gone.

I still hunt on wild, windy autumn days when the maple and poplar leaves swirl among the snowflakes, and in other seasons I dream of such days: the dog at my side, the blustery gusts of early winter pushing the northern ducks south from the arctic, seeking shelter, their legs outstretched and wings set. They coast and glide and brake, hissing in close to wheel over the decoys. In my dream I rarely rise and shoot. Instead, I hunch lower in the blind and watch the horizon, anticipating the unrestrained wildness of the next flock, undivided from the next dream, or from the next time I awake before first light and listen for the wind.

KILLER FIRST DATE
by Allison Gorner

Vivian pulled the keys from the ignition and glanced at the clock. Five minutes early. Her stomach did a little flip of anticipation. She could scope it out, see if he was there. Don't want to seem too eager, though. She took a big breath, forcing herself to calm. Better not go in yet. Best to be exactly punctual, like always. That would give the right impression. Interested. Not eager.

Four more minutes. To pass the time, Vivian checked her phone, scanning the headlines.

Prime Minister Attends UN Summit
Body Found on Calgary River Bank
- Police Suggest Link to Three Unsolved

Deaths

Maybe this date was a bad idea. She scrolled down some more.

The River Killer Strikes Again
Serial Killer on the Loose

A terrible, awful idea. What kind of risk was she getting herself into? Right now, a bloated, soggy corpse lay in the morgue and the police were searching for a serial killer.

The thought of killers and corpses brought back the image of a young woman, Jane, her last patient of the day. Face bruised blue and purple, and her shoulder hanging at an unnatural angle, Jane had arrived at the clinic where Vivian worked as a nurse. Vivian helped her out of her ragged clothes and into a hospital gown. She took pictures of the injuries, collected swabs, and bagged the clothes as evidence, all while Jane stared unfocused and unmoving as if she were already dead.

Someone had done that to her. Someone who spoke of supposed love, but instead acted in rage and violence. Vivian urged her to press charges because, next time this happened, it would most likely be the last. Jane had disagreed and the case was dropped.

Vivian struggled to leave her work at the clinic without bringing it home. It ate her up inside, knowing the limitations of her profession in helping women like Jane. She never felt like she did enough for her patients. She took another big breath, pushed the memory away, and closed the headlines. It wouldn't do to dwell on her patients, and on bodies and murderers right now.

Instead she opened his profile. Theodore B. Talbot, with his blonde hair, blue eyes, six-pack abs, and debonair smile, looked like the quintessential A-list movie star. At least his picture did. He listed his hobbies as going to the gym, volunteering at the homeless shelter, and visiting his grandma. Was he really like that? He sounded perfect. A little too perfect. Then again, didn't all dating profiles sound that way?

She was a bit surprised when he sent a meet request. He had the look of a guy who wouldn't settle for anyone less than an eight – only the chic and exquisite. She wasn't exactly up to the movie star standard. With hair the same shade as a UPS truck, last year's fashions, and a figure a little beyond curvy, Vivian felt more drab than elegant. Her resentful temper didn't help either. Her stepdad used to call her *Vicious Viv*, or *Viv The Vast*, but he was a colossal jerk. She'd lost fifty pounds since then and her stepdad wasn't around anymore. But all that wasn't exactly in her dating profile. Maybe she sounded perfect online too. She sure tried to make it alluring. It was simply her old insecurities popping up again—her old image of herself still ingrained in her head. Viv the Vast no longer existed. Gone was the insecure teenager that trembled every time her stepdad entered the room. Now, she was an independent, intelligent woman who stood up for herself and tried to inspire other women do the same. Her tenacity radiated across her profile, and a lot of men were attracted to that. A lot of men also liked a full figure and she did get a considerable amount of meet requests. But the moment she saw the request from Theodore B. Talbot, and his stunning blue eyes, she agreed to meet.

Should she calm her worries and hazard a meet, despite the headlines? Vivian glanced through the Timmie's window in front of her. Good, it was moderately busy—enough people to notice if he made a scene, to provide some protection. A buffer of sorts.

One minute to go. Vivian grabbed her

purse from the front seat and got out of the car. She hesitated. Perhaps she shouldn't risk it and just leave. She willed herself to calm.

Breathe.

Her breath expelled in little white clouds, hovering in the brisk air. Indecisive, she stood there another thirty seconds. Her fingers were getting cold. Inside would be heated and she could wrap them around a steaming cup of hot chocolate, extra whipped cream, and get warm. If he wasn't there by the time she got her order, she'd leave. If he was, well, then she'd talk to him.

Vivian walked inside and immediately the rich aroma of coffee and donuts filled her nostrils, easing her anxiety a little. She glanced around for Theodore. No sign of the beautiful blonde tresses yet. After ordering her drink, she moved to the end of the counter, awaiting its fulfillment. She took out her phone and debated whether to scroll through the headlines again when the barista interrupted her deliberation by placing a steaming cup near the edge of the counter. She pocketed her phone and took a step forward.

"Hot chocolate, extra whipped cream, for uh…" The barista paused glancing down at the receipt. "…Theodore!"

"That's me, thanks," a deep voice said behind her.

Surprised, Vivian turned to see blonde-haired, blue-eyed, presumably six-packed, Theodore B. Talbot. Just like his picture. Completely gorgeous. He grabbed his hot chocolate and leaned toward Vivian.

"Hi," he said with a smile, displaying his impeccable white teeth.

"Hi," she managed to squeak out, her voice breaking. Vivian blushed. She didn't normally react to men like this. It was a source of pride that she kept her reactions in control, and she had worked diligently for a long time to do so. But he really was very attractive.

Breathe. Relax.

"You must be…"

"Vivian!" the barista interrupted once more. "Hot chocolate, extra whipped cream."

"Vivian. A perfect match." He tilted his head endearingly toward the hot chocolate and smiled again. "And my date."

"Umm, yes. The date… I mean, yes, I'm your date." She needed to salvage her control. "And you are Theodore."

"Guilty, as charged. Shall we sit? I claimed a table over here."

Theodore indicated the way with a gallant, yet goofy, wave of his arm, seized Vivian's drink for her and led the way. He set the drinks on the table and pulled out a chair for her.

"Thanks," Vivian said, impressed by his gentlemanly behaviour. Few dates operated that way anymore. At least not any men she had dated. Pleased, she accepted his polite offer and sat, placing her purse in her lap.

Theodore sat across from her, took a big slurp of his hot chocolate and whipped cream, and gave a contented sigh.

"Nothing like sugar-on-sugar, am I right?" His eyes crinkled in the corner as he grinned. "I can't do coffee anymore. Gives me the jitters. How about you?"

"I like my coffee black, but today seemed like a sugar-on-sugar kind of day."

"Yeah, I know what you mean," he said staring out the window. "It's a little terrifying out there. Or soon will be."

"What do you mean?" Vivian wrapped her hands tighter around her cup. Although her fingers were back to their normal temperature, she still felt an inner chill.

"Terrifying. It's supposed to get to minus forty tonight. Hopefully, no one gets stuck out there in the cold. People have died, you know."

They sat in silence for a moment,

Theodore distracted, Vivian nervous. What was he thinking about? The body found by the river? She was definitely thinking about that body. Cold and dead. She fiddled with the zipper on her purse, opening and closing it several times. The harsh sound seemed to bring Theodore out of his contemplation. He pulled his gaze away from the chilly parking lot and looked at Vivian. Annoyance flashed in his eyes for a brief instant—or was it anger—and then disappeared just as quickly. She must have imagined it.

"Sorry, just thinking about what I need to do before it gets too cold," he said and smiled, all traces of anger gone. "I better stop by the shelter tonight. Make sure they have enough blankets."

Blankets. He was thinking about blankets for the homeless, not bodies. She let go of some tension and felt her shoulders relax.

"So, what do you do for work, Theodore?" Vivian asked in an attempt to bring her thoughts back to normal first date conversation. "Or do you prefer Ted?"

"Call me Theo, not Ted—makes me think of Ted Bundy." He gave a little chuckle.

Vivian stared at him, dumbfounded. Why would he say that?

"You know. Ted Bundy. The serial killer…" he trailed off, embarrassed with Vivian's silence.

"I know who Ted Bundy is," Vivian asserted.

He must know something more about the serial killer on the loose. But that's ridiculous. Why would he know more about it than she did? She was being paranoid. He probably saw the news and had serial killers on the brain, just like the rest of the city. Just like her.

"Of course, you know who he is. Ted Bundy. Not the greatest person to talk about on a date. Especially when we barely know each other. Ted Bundy, the serial killer…" He trailed off as he recognized the hole he was digging himself into. "Finance," he blurted after a heavy pause. "To answer your question. I'm in finance. What do you do?"

This guy was kind of awkward, even if he was gorgeous.

"I'm a nurse."

"Any specialty?"

"Yes. I'm a forensic nurse."

Theodore stared at her for a moment, uncomprehending, which did not surprise Vivian. Forensic nursing was a specialty still in its infancy, and it often came as a surprise to people that she worked with crime victims to gather medical evidence and sometimes testified in court. The general population didn't even know her job existed, and it didn't look like Theodore was about to admit his ignorance on the subject.

"Oh. Cool," he said.

She was right.

This wasn't going as she'd hoped. He was

distracted and had bumbled his way through most of their conversation, but she hadn't exactly given off the approachable vibe, either. How would she know if she wanted to take this to the next step if she didn't shed her iciness and act more warmly to him? She needed to put the headlines aside and focus on Theo, the person. Time for control.

Breathe. Relax. Smile.

"Hey, Theo, I think we got off to a rocky start. I've been a little distracted. Do you want to try again?" Vivian gave him a sweet apologetic smile. She tucked her hair behind her ear, then grasped her purse, fingering the zipper pull absent-mindedly.

"Yeah, I'd like that," he said, running his fingers through his hair in relief. "I have this app that generates random ice-breaker questions. Interested? I know it's kind of nerdy..."

"No, that sounds fun."

Theo pulled out his phone and set it on the

table. Displayed in the centre of the screen was a round green button with the word PUSH.

"Ladies first."

Vivian tapped the button on the screen. The button disappeared and words materialized and slowly came into focus until a full sentence was legible.

"What was the worst haircut you ever had?" Vivian read. "Easy. Mushroom cut, ten years old."

"Seriously?" Theo chortled.

"Seriously! They were super in-style. I thought it would be awesome, but I regretted it the very next day." Vivian laughed too. "What, like you've never had one?"

"Never."

"I don't believe you," Vivian joked.

"It's true!"

"No mushroom cut? No bowl cut?"

"Bowl cuts are different," Theo insisted.

"Liar, they are not! You've had a mushroom

cut, and I bet it was just as bad as mine. No arguments. Your turn."

Vivian was enjoying their banter and felt herself relax. And when she was relaxed, she was in control. She needed to keep that control if she were to initiate the next step. Pretending to move closer to see the next question, Vivian laid one hand down on the table, her fingers millimeters away from Theo's. With the other hand, she silently zipped open her purse, reached inside and grasped a small bottle. Theo didn't notice as he tapped the screen and waited for a new question to appear, his fingers creeping ever closer to hers.

"What is the strangest thing that's ever happened to you?" he read. "Okay, I'll tell you, but you'll never believe it."

"Try me." Vivian pressed her thumb against the bottle lid, pushing it open.

"One morning, I'm fast asleep and I wake up to a S.W.A.T. team busting down my front door. They drag me out of bed and pin me to the floor. They're screaming and shouting and I'm so scared I almost pee my pants."

"Naturally," Vivian remarked as she clutched the bottle.

"This huge gorilla of a guy is yelling in my face, 'Theodore B. Talbot? Are you Theodore B. Talbot?' and I say, 'yeah' and he says, "Theodore Benjamin Talbot?' And I was so confused because my middle name is Brock, not Benjamin."

"There's two of you? Two Theodore B. Talbots?" Vivian closed the lid and dropped the bottle back in her purse.

"Yeah. Strange, right? It took a while to convince them I was a different Theodore Talbot than the one they wanted. I had to show them everything; birth certificate, passport, driver's license. It was a total crap show. But apparently this other guy was on some kind of watch list. Something to do with guns or bombs."

"Did they ever catch him?" she asked, inching her fingers away from Theo.

"No idea. One day some officer will tell my mom I've been found dead in a ditch somewhere, but it will really be this other dude, and it'll take forever to sort out."

"That is strange."

Scary even. Two Theodore B. Talbots. And the handsome Theo sitting near her was not the one she was looking for.

"This is fun. Do you want to try another question?" Theo asked. "We can both answer this time."

"Okay. Sure." Vivian zipped up her purse. It was about time to leave.

Theo pushed the button, and the next question appeared. *Who is your craziest ex?*

"I really haven't dated much," Vivian began, "so I don't have a big pool to draw from. But there was this one guy, Damien, who loved extreme sports. He would go bungee jumping, skydiving, base jumping, you name it. He said he loved the thrill. And he had a wicked temper. Too crazy for me."

"Me too. I have no desire to go skydiving. I'm more of a soccer kind of guy. Safe and sound on the ground." Theo smiled at his lame joke attempt and slid his fingers closer to Vivian again, narrowing the gap.

Vivian didn't move, but she could feel her control slipping a little. She wanted to stretch out her finger and touch his skin, to feel the warmth of his hand on hers. He wasn't the Theodore B. Talbot that enticed her here, but maybe this could be a normal date. Two people getting to know each other. No ulterior motives. No next step.

"My craziest ex," Theo continued, "was this super high-maintenance, naturally blonde yoga instructor. She was neurotic. One minute she was happy and bubbly, the next she was chucking things at me, telling me it was over. She was crazy."

"She does sound crazy."

"If you ever walk into a yoga class and the instructor's name is Meegan, turn around and never go back!"

Meegan. She knew that name, knew that face. It was forever seared into her memory. Like Jane, Meegan was a girl who came into the clinic where Vivian worked. The tall, blonde, fit girl who had bruises all over her body, a bloody gash on her forehead, and extensive internal bleeding. The girl whose boyfriend, Theodore B. Talbot, beat her up when she confronted him about his other lovers. The Theodore whose slick lawyers got him off with only mandated community service. Like volunteering at a homeless shelter. The girl who couldn't even talk about it because of the court's strict gag order, and who died two months later.

This *was* the Theodore B. Talbot she was looking for. Vivian's heart started racing. This man had a hidden darkness to him. A darkness that remained unchecked because of his good looks, easy demeanour, and deep pockets. It needed to be checked.

Control. She needed to regain her control.

Breathe. Relax. Smile. Charm.

"Meegan," Vivian said thoughtfully. "That's an unusual name. I met a Meegan once."

"Was she crazy?"

"She was definitely unbalanced when I met her." Vivian wiggled her fingers a bit, encouraging Theo to close the gap.

"Yeah, no more blondes for me." Theodore laughed. He accepted her unspoken invitation and brushed her pinkie with his.

"Luckily, I'm a brunette." She spread her fingers and intertwined them with Theo's, ignoring the icy shiver in her heart.

"I'm really enjoying this," Theodore said.

"Me too." Vivian lied. "Even with the rocky start."

"Do you want to get out of here? Grab a drink or go for a walk? It's not too cold yet."

"I'd love to go for a walk. I know a beautiful

trail by the river. The parking area is a lovely secluded lookout with great views of the city. And then we could…" Vivian leaned a little closer and let her words trail off.

"That's perfect." He cleared his throat, distracted by her flirtation.

"Perhaps we could drive separately and meet there," she suggested.

"Yes. I, uh… I just need to visit the washroom first, though. Unlike you, I drank all of my hot chocolate." Theodore reluctantly released Vivian's hand and stood.

"Would you like another?"

"I don't know. That's a lot of sugar."

"You only live once," she teased.

"You know what? I would. Why not? It's a sugar-on-sugar kind of day." Theodore grinned his movie-star grin and left the table.

Vivian also left the table and went to the counter. She ordered another overly sweet hot chocolate for her date (she never really liked sweet drinks) and a black coffee for herself. She stood at the end of the counter, again waiting for her order. Looking around to make sure Theodore was still in the washroom, Vivian opened her purse. She found the small bottle and opened the lid. She plucked out one miniature pill, hiding it in her hand, and returned the bottle to her purse. The barista announced her order just as Theodore returned to her side. Vivian quickly stepped forward, grabbed the drinks and discreetly dropped the pill into Theodore's hot chocolate, initiating the next step. She handed him his drink.

"Cheers," she said, and they both took a drink.

"Delicious. Thanks." Theodore moved to the exit and held the door open for Vivian, and they both stepped outside.

Theodore could put on a show of good manners, but his hidden inner rage made him rotten. Just like her stepdad and her ex, Damien. Like all the countless other men whose favourite pastime was beating up women. Women who came into her clinic every day, bloody and broken, with wounds no words could ever repair. Only definitive action could hope to bridge the gap between broken and healing. Ideally the action of the law, but that was a rare occurrence. When the law inevitably failed, it came down to her, Vivian, the only one with the guts to take vital action.

"Which way to the lookout?" Theodore asked. He pulled out his phone to plug in the directions and then grimaced. "Wow, did you hear about this? There's a serial killer on the loose. No wonder you were freaked out about my talk of Ted Bundy."

"I saw a few headlines," she said warily.

"Don't worry though, this guy, the killer, has only gone after men. No women. So, you're safe. In case you're worried…"

She was worried about the headlines, but not for the reason Theodore supposed. She was worried that she was taking too much risk meeting him tonight. Did the police suspect her? Was she being watched?

"It's okay. I never thought you were a serial killer," Vivian assured him, bringing her focus back to him. "What does the article say?"

"Just that three bodies have been found over the last eight months. They *may* be connected. Then again, may not be. They all have the same drug in their system— probably some new contaminated street drug. The police are being very vague and don't have any suspects. Except maybe someone blonde. Crazy blondes, right?" Theodore looked up at her and grinned.

Vivian nodded her assent. "Crazy blondes." Like Theodore.

Returning his attention to the news article, he continued reading. "They are being very clear that they don't think it's a serial killer, but of course that's the only phrase the media picked up on."

"That's horrible." She arranged a look of concern on her face. Inside, she was beaming. She wasn't a suspect. Even better, the police found only three bodies. They found none of the others yet. Vivian let out a slow breath she didn't realize she was holding.

The pill could prove problematic if they traced it back to her, but that didn't seem likely. Her precautions had been considerable, bordering on the extreme. She could sell some of her stash and get it out on the street, let the police have a rationale to continue investigating the fake trail. Vivian was getting ahead of herself. She could work out the pill complication later. Right now, she needed to focus on her date. On this gorgeous man with the movie star looks, who trusted her. This man who destroyed a beautiful girl named Meegan and got away with it. Whose limbs would quit working in about twenty minutes. Soon after that, his heart would quit too.

It was a shame, really. He was exquisite. And for a moment earlier, she hoped he was the wrong Theodore B. Talbot. It would've been fun to flirt with a man who would be alive the next day to remember it.

"Here," Vivian said as she moved closer to Theodore, inclining her body toward his. "Let me enter the directions for you." She wrapped her fingers around his hand, slid the phone out of his palm and typed in the address. She returned the phone and allowed her hand to linger, caressing his fingers as she pulled away.

"I'll meet you there," Theodore said, his voice low and eager.

"You go ahead. I need to visit the ladies' room first. When you get to the lookout, will you wait for me?" she implored.

"Definitely."

Vivian stepped inside as Theodore pulled out of the parking lot. As always, she remained hyper-aware of the security camera, angling her face so it never had a perfect view of her. But she wanted to make sure she was observed at this moment, albeit partially, not leaving with Theodore B. Talbot. Once inside the ladies' room, she deadbolted the door and stepped in front of the mirror. She carefully took off her UPS-brown wig and set it on the counter. Her naturally blonde hair was pinned tightly to her scalp, except for one lock that had wriggled loose. She refastened the stray lock and returned the wig to her head. Perfect.

Vivian returned to her car and checked the clock. By the time she arrived at the lookout, the pill would have taken effect and Theodore should be immobilized. All she would need to do is watch and wait for his heart to stop. Then she'd take his phone, put his car in gear and let it roll forward to get lost in the depths of the frigid river. And justice would be satisfied. Justice for all battered women. Justice for Meegan.

It was time to complete the last step of this killer first date. Vivian turned the key in the ignition and her heart raced. Control.

Breathe. Relax. Smile. Charm.

Kill.

RAIN, DRIZZLE AND FOG
by Bronwynn Erskine

Heather tucked her chin deeper into her jacket's collar as she descended the steep curve of McBride's Hill and tried her best to ignore the mural that loomed accusingly over her. Memorialising the Great Fire of 1892 that had destroyed most of downtown St John's, it always made her self-conscious. As if her adopted city wanted to remind her it was watching. She shivered, as much at the cold fog rolling in off the harbour as at the ominous thought, and hurried down onto Water Street. In her pocket, her fingers curled of their own accord to trace the burn scar at the base of her thumb.

There was little traffic and almost no pedestrians at this hour on a Saturday

131

morning. Heather was grateful for that. She desperately wanted some peace after being kept up half the night listening to her roommate's enthusiastic and extremely vocal bedroom escapades.

When she reached Rocket Bakery, it too was largely quiet. She splurged on a currant-laced scone to go with her coffee, dosed the mug liberally with cream and sugar, and headed into the café seating area where the mismatched furniture reminded her comfortingly of her great-grandmother's farm.

Only one table was occupied at the moment. A Black woman with exquisitely applied gold eyeliner gestured expansively, making her rings and bracelets glitter and flash like rainbow scales as she spoke. Her companion, an Asian woman whose pointed face was framed by chunky amber highlights in her bobbed hair, listened with focused attention. There was an empty chair at their table and, just for a moment, Heather indulged herself in the fantasy of being the sort of person who might walk up and ask to join them.

With a purely internal sigh, she settled alone at her favourite table in the window corner instead. However it was one made friends as an adult, Heather hadn't mastered it yet. She pulled out her laptop and logged into the café Wi-Fi, hoping to drown her loneliness with school work.

As she tried to immerse herself in research for her paper on the architecture of Versailles, she couldn't help stealing covert glances at the other table. Her fingers itched for her sketchbook. Both women had such expressive faces that would be delightful to draw. She wondered whether she'd be able to capture the texture of the Black woman's broad afro, and made a mental note to find some reference pictures online later of people with similar hairstyles to try drawing from. There were so many things she'd never thought to try, growing up in an almost entirely white neighbourhood. She hadn't realised how many until she went away to university.

She couldn't get her focus to settle on her research paper this morning, in spite of being interested in the topic when she'd chosen it only the week before. Her mind kept wandering off on unhelpful little tangents.

When another woman strolled into the café, Heather's focus fell apart completely. Tall and umber-skinned (First Nations perhaps? Heather wasn't sure), she had a generous figure that would not have been out of place in a Rubens painting and wore a long sealskin coat over a short pencil skirt and chunky boots.

"Hey stranger. How was your trip?" the Black woman called as she leapt up to embrace the new arrival.

"You know how family is," she replied with a laugh far brighter than the grey light straining to make it through the clouds outside. "It's nice to go and see them, and even nicer to leave again."

Heather wanted to do so much more than sketch her. She thought of watercolours and oils, of tracing a paintbrush around the curves of thigh and throat. Her skin felt hot with a blush that was surely very visible against her fair complexion. Heat curled around the back of her neck, and she was painfully aware of every bit of herself.

When she caught a faint whiff of wood smoke, she knew she needed to leave.

She swallowed the last few mouthfuls of coffee as she carried her mug over to the dirty dishes tray. On the way back, she passed the three women chatting around their own table and noticed that the newcomer's lovely coat had slipped and pooled on the floor.

"Oh, you dropped your coat," Heather said, stooping to pick it up and drape it across the back of the woman's chair. "There you go. Don't want it getting dirty."

The woman gave her a startled look and reached up to touch the coat protectively. The intensity in her dark eyes made Heather flush more deeply, and something hot and bright unfurled under her ribs.

"I, I didn't mean to interrupt," Heather stammered, taking a quick step back. She grabbed up her computer and her backpack, and fled the café.

Outside, the fog had thickened to drizzle. The cool dampness of it was a relief, but not enough to cool her furious blush or help her recover her composure. Cursing under her breath, she awkwardly stuffed the laptop into her bag and zipped it up tight before jogging down the street to the bus stop.

The heat in her chest stubbornly refused to subside as she wrapped her arms around herself and huddled under the shallow overhang of a closed storefront. She could feel her heart beating, and if anything, the scent of wood smoke had gotten stronger. Closing her eyes, she forced herself to take slow, deep breaths as her therapist had suggested to help with the panic attacks. She could only hope they would help with this as well.

She was still struggling to calm herself down when the scent of wood smoke was swept away by a gust of wind redolent with the smell of the sea.

"You look nervous," the sea air purred.

Heather yelped, eyes snapping open again to find the woman in the sealskin coat stood only a metre away. Water beaded on the fur of her coat and on her long, dark lashes, but the rain didn't seem to trouble her.

"I. What?" Heather asked, trying not to gape. Or to stop breathing entirely and die of embarrassment.

The other woman graced her with that smile, dazzling as sunlight on the sea, and repeated "You seem nervous. You left before I could thank you, so it can't have been something I said."

Heather's blush was back again in full force. "I'm just, y'know, an awkward person. Nervous just in general," she said, stumbling over her own tongue in a way that surely added veracity to the comment. "There's really no need to thank me just for picking up your coat."

One hand, adorned with three silver rings, rose to touch the coat again and her smile grew charged with some emotion Heather couldn't read. "The coat has a great deal of meaning to me," she murmured.

"It's very pretty," Heather said shyly.

It was. Darker greys dappled the paler base colour like a constellation of freckles, and Heather found her mind wandering to the other woman's smooth skin. A spray of freckles traced the line of one broad cheekbone, and she wondered if there were other freckles she couldn't see. The heat in her chest surged again.

"So are you," the stranger replied, leaning in closer. "I'm Morgan."

"H-Heather," Heather whispered. The smell of wood smoke was back in her nostrils and her fingertips tingled with a telltale warmth. She needed to leave before she did something awful, but she couldn't bring herself to step back from Morgan's intoxicating presence.

"Why don't you come back inside and have coffee with us, Heather?" Morgan invited. Still smiling, still leaning in close enough that Heather could hear the faint, musical rustling of her elaborate silver earrings.

"I, I shouldn't."

Morgan arched a brow and tilted her head. "Why ever not? Do you have somewhere else to be? I'd like to get to know you."

"I can't." Heather could not possibly have blushed more deeply. Her whole body felt scorched with it. She managed to stumble back a step and raise a hand between them, but was horrified to see thin curls of smoke rising from her fingertips into the cool air.

"That's something you don't see every day," Morgan mused. Her tone was calm and curious, not at all what Heather would have expected if she'd had the time to think on it.

But Heather couldn't take her eyes off the thickening smoke and the way light was beginning to flicker over the surface of her pink polished nails. "I have to go," she whispered tremulously, but she couldn't make her body move.

"Please don't, darling."

Gently, as if she was handling delicate crystal, Morgan cradled Heather's hand between both of her own and raised it to her lips. She kissed the pad of each smoking finger with deliciously cool lips, all the while keeping her eyes locked with Heather's. When she'd finished, the breath she exhaled was laden with cool, sea scented fog.

Heather could only stare as the burning heat curled sullenly back in on itself until there was nothing in her chest except her wildly beating heart.

"There now, that's better. Why don't you come on back inside? You look like a stiff breeze would blow you over right now, and we can't have that," Morgan said, wrapping an arm around Heather's shoulders and drawing her, unresisting, back towards the café.

The sealskin coat brushed against the nape of Heather's neck as they walked, making her insides tremble. She was desperately afraid the fire would come back, but it remained quiescent for the moment. Being wrapped in the ocean wind scent of Morgan's presence seemed to calm it somehow.

Heather was barely aware of the half block walk back until she found herself being pressed down into a chair across from one of Morgan's friends.

"This is Heather," Morgan was saying. She kept a hand on Heather's shoulder as she leaned back to swipe a chair from another table and bring it around to seat herself. "Heather, this is Hsin-yi."

Hsin-yi's choppy bangs trailed forward to half-conceal the mischievous glint in her eyes. "Good to meet you," she said in a deceptively calm tone. "What do you think of a winter wedding?"

"Be nice," Morgan muttered.

Heather shrugged. "Winter's nice, I guess. Who's getting married?"

Morgan was positively glaring at her friend now. "Don't," she warned.

Ignoring her, Hsin-yi raised her coffee cup to her lips in a way that didn't quite hide her growing smirk. "She didn't tell you?"

"Tell me what?" Heather asked, glancing helplessly between the two women as she tried to figure out what she'd been dragged into.

"That she's a selkie? That you have to marry her now? Anything about the coat? She really didn't tell you?" Hsin-yi was trying to affect an innocent expression, but the curl of her lips gave her away.

"Don't listen to her," Morgan put in hastily. "You're terrible. I don't know why I hang out with you."

"What, you've got to tell your lovely bride."

Heather's emotions roiled so fervently that she could feel the heat starting to wake in her chest again. Surely, they'd noticed her blushing and this was an exercise in mockery. Panic fanned the flames awake more quickly than embarrassment.

"Stop," Morgan growled. The tone was so harsh it knocked the teasing smile from her friend's face. When she turned towards Heather, her expression softened again.

"What?" Heather tried to ask, but stuttered

143

to a halt when she tasted wood smoke in the back of her throat.

Morgan took her trembling hands again and leaned in until her breath caressed Heather's cheek. "Stop," she repeated far more gently. Her voice was a cool swirl of fog and her eyes were drowning-deep. "Just breathe. You're alright."

It took longer for the heat to recede this time. Heather could feel herself trembling, but Morgan's fingers curled through her own gave her a sort of anchor that kept her from dissolving completely into a panic attack. Slowly, breath by breath, the heat settled back into a sullen smoulder.

"I, I should go," Heather whispered, voice trembling. "It's not, I mean I'm not safe when I'm like this. To be around."

Morgan leaned in a little closer and rested their foreheads together. "Please stay a bit longer. I won't let anything happen to you."

The certainty in her voice made Heather's

resolve wobble. "You don't know..."

"I know you're a baby firestarter," Morgan cut in gently. "I've never met one before, but I'm familiar with the magic. I promise, I can and will keep your power from getting out of control."

Heather could only stare. Her voice felt locked away in her throat, as it did sometimes when the anxiety overwhelmed her, and she could feel tears gathering at the corners of her eyes.

Morgan freed a hand to brush the tears away. "Shh, it's alright. I promise. I'll help you find someone who can teach you control. It'll be okay."

Breath hitching in something that wasn't quite a sob, Heather ducked her head away. "Everyone thought. I mean, I couldn't. When it started happening. No one believed me that it was." Her words stumbled to a halt, tangled hopelessly in each other.

"Hardly anyone believes in magic

anymore," Morgan agreed, catching the gist of the stuttered sentences. She curled her fingers into Heather's frazzled pixie cut and guided her face down into the curve of her neck. The hug was tight and sure, and her skin, like her breath, smelled faintly of the sea.

Heather breathed her in and let the tears come. When she'd first moved to St John's, she'd stood beside the harbour and breathed in the briny, fishy smell of the sea, and tried to convince herself that she would be safe here. The salt scent of Morgan's skin gave her back some of the confidence she'd tried to instil in herself that day.

When she finally pulled away, Morgan's fingers lingered in her hair and along the nape of her neck. Cool, delicious shivers followed in their wake.

"Sorry," Heather muttered, skin flushing all over again with the realisation that she'd just been crying on the shoulder of a woman who was the next thing to a stranger.

Morgan chuckled and reached past her to snag a purse embroidered with brightly coloured snakes that hung over the back of the empty chair next to her. "Don't be," she replied cheerfully, riffling through the purse and coming up with a package of makeup wipes. "Let's get you cleaned up before my supposed friends come back."

With deft, practiced strokes, Morgan cleaned away the eyeliner and shadow she'd worked so hard to get right. It hadn't been very good to begin with, and Heather was sure her tears had smudged it out of all recognition. The makeup wipe left her skin cool and faintly tingling. Or maybe that was from Morgan's touch again. She swallowed hard.

"There, no more raccoon eyes," Morgan said.

"At least not until next time I put makeup on," Heather replied. She glanced up through her lashes and tried to find something to say.

Morgan laughed and her face lit up again like sunlight sparking across the surface of the waves. "It's just a matter of practice. Laila can probably give you some pointers if she ever comes back."

"I heard my name. What am I giving pointers on?" a voice called across the café.

When Heather looked over her shoulder, she found the Black woman from earlier approaching along with Hsin-yi, who looked rather apologetic now.

"Makeup," Morgan replied without missing a beat. "Heather, this is Laila. Laila, Heather. And I stole makeup wipes out of your purse 'cause I don't have any on me."

"No worries, and my favourite subject," Laila replied. She reached the table and set down a miniature cake crowned with delicate blue icing flowers and the word 'Congratulations!' in bright, sinuous green. "I'd already bought the cake before Hsin-yi warned me. So, we can just eat it and not talk about the whole selkie marriage thing."

"You're awful. Remind me again why I'm friends with you two?" Morgan said with a sigh.

Laila shrugged and began passing around plates and forks. "Because we're awesome," she replied.

"Because you're also awful," Hsin-yi suggested. She gave Heather a regretful smile and added "Sorry for earlier. Teasing Morgan's all well and good, but it was a dick move to drag you into it like that. Friends?"

Heather returned the smile. "Sure, friends," she agreed. "I don't really have any of those here yet."

"Well, you've got us as friends now," Morgan said. She hesitated, actually starting to blush herself, and her knee bumped against Heather's. "And maybe more than friends."

Heather was still gaping, open-mouthed

and fishlike, when Laila thumped a big slice of cake down on her plate and announced "Selkie aren't very subtle. Like, at all. Ever."

Jumping a little, Heather glanced up at her. "I thought you were going to stop teasing," she whispered.

Hsin-yi rolled her eyes and swiped the knife out of Laila's hand to cut herself a more reasonably sized slice. "Nah, that part wasn't teasing. Morgan is a selkie."

"What? But that's just, folk stories and stuff isn't it?" Heather asked, turning her gaze between the two with a frown.

Morgan's smile was a little teasing and a little nervous at the same time. "Says the woman with fire in her chest," she replied. With a faint shrug, she added, "Like I said, not many people believe in magic anymore, but it's still around. The coat thing isn't true though."

"So, you can't turn into a seal by putting it on?" Heather asked. She was startled to

150

realise she was a little disappointed.

"Oh no, that's true. But not the marriage part." Morgan trailed off and glanced away, definitely blushing now.

"She means returning her coat to her doesn't make you her wife," Laila supplied with a grin that was suspiciously pleased for someone who'd promised to refrain from teasing.

"Yeah, that," Morgan muttered, sending her friend a glare. "It's a really old-fashioned idea that I never should have told my nosey friends about."

Heather wasn't sure what she felt, but there was a little corner of herself that suggested *disappointment* wouldn't be out of line.

"Yeah, super old-fashioned," Laila continued cheerfully. "It's more like an engagement now."

"Only if you wanted it to be," Morgan hurried to assure.

Heather's heart leapt and her chest filled with heat that she didn't think was related to the fire at all. She knew her eyes must be very wide and her cheeks very red, but for once, her nerves didn't tangle her words. "I think maybe I do," she whispered.

THE SISTERHOOD
by Joan Baril

The family secret was slipping out. At sixteen, I reacted with intense embarrassment. I didn't realize that another secret, more intense and more interesting, was also hiding close by.

In 1955, I worked Saturdays at the boys' department in Eaton's. When the closing bell shrilled, my cousin Bubsie (who I had to call Miss Reitman in the store) and I began straightening the stacks of sweaters and bush jackets on the wooden counters and covering them with long blue drop cloths.

Just to make conversation, and because I knew Bubsie was familiar with the family secret, I said, "I'm going with my mother over to Miss O'Shea's tomorrow afternoon. She

153

lost her engagement ring."

Bubsie's hands flew to her face and the pile of boys' wool socks she was carrying flipped in a cascading arc. "What in God's name are you talking about, Janet?" She didn't pick up the socks. Instead, she stared at me, one hand on the counter as if for support.

"Miss O'Shea's my algebra teacher," I said.

"I know that," Bubsie snapped. "What the hell is this about an engagement ring? Surely you are not telling me that Mary Margaret O'Shea is engaged?"

"Oh, yes," I said, "But she's lost the..."

"Hold your horses," Bubsie barked, flinging both palms toward me. Then, she stooped for the shirts, flinging them roughly on the counter. She grabbed the cotton cover that I was holding and flipped it over the merchandise. "I'll organize when I come in on Monday."

I was speechless. Bubsie was an exacting

154

boss, and insisted on a rigid closing-time routine. Everything had to be in order before we left the floor.

"OK, OK," she said, her voice trembling. "This is what we're going to do. I'll take you out for supper. OK? How about a Stan-and-Sy at the Arthur Café? Phone your mother and tell her."

I nodded, too surprised to reply. But I loved the gravy-laden hot sandwiches at the café across the street and a Stan-and-Sy was certainly better than the creamed peas on toast waiting at home.

A quarter of an hour later, I was sitting in a booth, trying to think of calming words, although I had no idea why my news had agitated Bubsie.

"Miss O'Shea came to our house last night," I slowly started in. "She said she'd lost her engagement ring. It's got two diamonds. She's sure it's somewhere in her suite. She says she's never worn it in public yet. She's

155

only been engaged for a week. She said she'd heard about my mother and came for help."

I blushed. My mother's ability to find lost objects made me squirm with mortification. Both my mother and Bubsie's mother, my Aunt Sissy, had inherited the so-called *Gift*. They also saw the future in tea leaves. However, these facts were seldom mentioned outside the family circle. This suited me fine. I cringed to think what the kids at Port Arthur Collegiate would say if they learned my mother was psychic.

But unfortunately, some rumours must have slithered out. Witness Miss O'Shea's visit.

Bubsie poured the tea from the brown crockery pot. "Did she say who she is engaged to?"

"Mr. Muir, the physics teacher."

"Never heard of him," Bubsie said. Then she added, "The poor sap."

I could not figure Bubsie out at all. "I think it's wonderful," I said stoutly. "Now she won't be an old maid anymore. She probably thought she'd never get married because she's pretty old."

The waitress lowered the Stan-and-Sy in front of me. It was a six-inch tall layered concoction of white bread, roast pork and sliced onion awash in thick brown gravy. A two-inch high dike of French-fried potatoes circled the edge of the plate.

I breathed in the mesmerizing richness of gravy and fat and, leaning over, took up my knife and fork.

Bubsie was frowning and shaking her head, but she turned to the waitress. "Alma, would you bring me a salt fish sandwich on rye please. And more hot water for the tea."

"Mary Margaret O'Shea is thirty-four," said Bubsie to me, emphasizing each word. "That is *not old* Janet. And there are worse things than being an old maid."

157

"Such as?" I said, shaking vinegar on the fries.

"Marrying someone you don't love for one thing. Marrying a man when you are not suited to it. Marrying so your religious family will be happy and shut up about it. Marrying because you think it's the right thing to do."

I was indignant. "That's not fair, Bubsie," I said. "You don't know that."

"Look," said Bubsie, "do you know the bookkeeper at Eaton's, Elaine Gatherum? She lives with Mary Margaret O'Shea and has done so for the last ten years. How do you think she feels about this engagement?"

I shrugged. I only knew the bookkeeper to say hello and I didn't even know Miss O'Shea very well outside of school. "I think she'd be happy to see her friend married at last," I said.

Bubsie sighed. She looked at her open-faced sandwich and pushed it away. But then she pulled it back, took several paper

158

serviettes from the holder, wrapped the sandwich carefully and put it in her purse.

"OK, Janet, I'm off. I can't make you see any more than that. I'll pay the bill and you finish up that monstrosity. Do you want Boston Cream Pie for dessert?"

I nodded, taking a big forkful of sandwich. "Oh, thank you Bubsie," I said. Gravy runnelled down my chin. "This is wonderful."

~ ~ ~

The next afternoon, as my mother and I walked the two blocks to Miss O'Shea's place, my mother grumbled. "I must be daft Janet. I should 'ave said to her right out, 'G'wan with ye, I have nay time for foolishness, losing your ring in your own house. Rank carelessness.' But I'm too polite, I am."

I said nothing, afraid she would turn back.

Originally, I had begged to go because I had heard at school that Miss O'Shea's suite was decorated in the new light Scandinavian style and I was dying to see it. My plan, when I married, was to have all light colours in my own place. But it was impossible not to mull over Bubsie's mysterious hints that had me speculating on the whole affair.

My mother was still grumbling. "Mind, if she pushes university for you again, I'll leave."

I winced. A year ago, when I was in Grade 11, Miss O'Shea had come over to our house one evening to talk about me and suggest I was a good candidate for university. My mother had just laughed and smiled and made tea and set out the scones, but later she rounded on me. "What is it with you? This is the second teacher planting ideas in your head." My Grade 8 teacher, Miss Joliette, also had mentioned university one time when she had met my mother on the street. "You attract all these old biddies. A bright lass you are, indeed. University! Huh! Who pays for that, eh?"

Before we could knock, Miss O'Shea opened the door of her third-floor suite. She must have heard us coming up the stairs. "Oh, so good of you to come, Mrs. Marsden," she said. Her eyes were puffed into slits behind her glasses and her face was so splotched she looked like a spotted apple. Her reddish hair stuck up around her head like a caragana bush in a high wind.

Arms out, she swooped toward us capturing both my mother's hands in hers. She held them up as if they were precious objects and rocked them back and forth. My mother's face fell into astonished stone. For a dreadful second, I thought Miss O'Shea was going to clutch my mother's hands to her rounded bosom or, even worse, fling her arms around my mother and cry on her shoulder. It would be the end of the visit, I knew. We would be out the door and down

161

the stairs and I would hear about nothing else for weeks.

"Oh, so good, so good to help me, Mrs. Marsden." She rocked. Every word had a little sobbing stutter in it. "I've searched everywhere. I can't look anymore, I can't do it..." Her lip quivered as if she were gasping for air.

I couldn't look at her. I'd never seen a teacher cry before; I felt my toes curdle. My mother snatched away her hands. Even though I knew my mother wanted to say, "Don't blether, for heaven's sake," she pasted on a ghastly smile. "Shall we make a start?" she said through clenched teeth.

"Of course, of course." Miss O'Shea took a hanky from her sleeve and wiped her eyes. She indicated the way into the living room. "I put those things out." A small velvet box and a picture of a ring cut from the Eaton's catalogue sat on the pale plastic coffee table. "Maybe they will help." Her voice snuffled, but she was trying hard for a smile. "Janet, would you like a glass of milk? Should I put the kettle on? To read the tea leaves perhaps?"

My mother shook her head and sat down on the grey sofa, first pushing away some towels that were tumbled there. She put her purse on the floor beside her. She picked up the blue velvet case, opened it and stared at the empty interior, snapped it closed and turned it round and round in her hand. She looked down at the small paper with the picture of the ring, but did not pick it up.

"I never wore it," Miss O'Shea faltered. "Not once. I never took it outside. It must be in here somewhere. I've looked…"

"Do shush," said my mother, "and sit down."

Miss O'Shea sat.

I was so nervous of my mother's temper I could not enjoy the Scandinavian living room. For one thing it was in a mess. Half the

163

books in the beige wooden bookcase were spilled out on the floor or piled on the grey carpet. On the pink walls, here and there, were lighter coloured squares as if someone had removed the pictures. Even the pale grey easy chairs and sofa with their wooden arms were littered in clothes, which we had to push aside to sit down. More piles of clothes were on the plastic end tables. On the table beside me, the pink ceramic heads of two flamingos poked through a jumble of rayon underpants. *Teacher underpants*! I did not know which way to look.

I wanted to ask many questions, but I dared not open my mouth. I knew my mother would shush me as sharply as she had shushed the algebra teacher. Nancy Drew was never told to shush, I raged inwardly. Neither was Miss Marple. They could ask questions whenever they wanted. For example, where was Miss Gatherum, the jealous roommate? Did my mother even know she existed? Had the bookkeeper grabbed all her stuff and books and pictures and stormed away, green-eyed and frothing over Miss O'Shea's good luck at catching a man? Obviously, the roommate was the culprit. She could have taken the ring and disposed of it anywhere. Flushed it down the toilet. Tossed it out the window into the snow. Taken it to Eaton's and hid it among the merchandise for a lucky customer to find.

"Uh huh," my mother said. Whenever my mother attempted to locate a lost object, she did not go into a trance or sway back and forth, or do any kind of fortune-teller routine. She just sat and, as she often told me, the idea would come, or it would not. I had once overheard her say to my Aunt Sissy, "We're both a wee bit fey, Sissy, 'tis true, but we have nay idea where it comes from for a' that. Thank God our girls have not inherited the Gift."

Now my mother stood up abruptly and

headed for the front hall. Miss O'Shea and I immediately followed. "You're right. It's in this suite somewhere." She reached into the closet and, taking out my coat, tossed it to me and then took down her own. Over her shoulder she said, "It could be in the kitchen." She opened the front door, and sat on the top step to put her overshoes on. I waited behind her until she had finished.

Miss O'Shea seemed unable to speak, but she followed the retreating back down the stairs. "But I've looked, I've looked," she called. "I can't look anymore…"

A dozen steps down, my mother turned and I thought I saw some sort of expression on her face. Was it possible it was sympathy? "Our Janet will stay and help you then," she said.

"What, me?" I cried. My mother shot me a glare as she disappeared around the bend in the stairs. I yanked off the overshoe that I'd been pulling on and stood up.

Miss O'Shea opened the kitchen door and beckoned me forward. Piles of dishes took up most of the table.

I scanned the room. Every cupboard door and drawer stood open. The counter was covered with pots and cooking gear. What a hodge-podge. But, first things first. I must ask my questions, discreetly of course, in good Jane Marple fashion. Instead, it all came out in a big blurt. "Where is Miss Gatherum anyway? She probably snaffled the ring. Out of spite, no doubt."

Miss O'Shea did not answer. She walked to the window and looked out at the snow-covered world below. "She's gone Janet, OK? That's all I know. I haven't a clue where she is. She has an aunt in Winnipeg and she might've gone there, but I don't know. Her car's gone too. And she put the ring case on the coffee table, just as you and your mother saw it. Empty."

I opened my mouth, but she headed off my

next remark. "And no, I don't think she took it with her. I know her very well. She's the kindest, most loving person. Anyway, your mother said it's around here somewhere, so..."

She turned from the window, her eyes hard and bleak. "But, that's not the problem, Janet. The problem is Tom Muir. He suspects, well he has heard, well he suspects a lot of things. When Elaine left, I couldn't see him; I haven't seen him for days. He probably thinks.... Hell, I don't know what he thinks and I don't care right now. But if I don't wear the ring, you see, and make it public..."

I didn't understand at all. "What? What will happen?"

"If I don't make it public, I might change my mind and I don't want to do that."

"Oh," I said.

Miss O'Shea sat down, shoulders slumped. "My good friends are mad at me for what I'm doing. We're like a sisterhood, and in this small town we stick together. We have to. It's a bit like a family; we're so loyal to each other. All my friends knew I loved Elaine, and I did love her. You have to understand. Sometimes women do. So, the sisterhood feels, oh I don't know if I can explain, but they feel sad. Yes, I think they feel a bit sad about it."

"Oh," I said again. I knew I was learning something important, something grown-up, but I was not sure what. My cousin, Bubsie, would explain, I thought. Bubsie knows everything. I'll leave the questions for her.

"Right," Miss O'Shea sighed. "Let's get on with it, shall we? You search the Frigidaire, Janet. I haven't looked in there yet."

I looked at the fridge. "It's not in there," I said. With these words, a soft tremor passed through me like a shiver of wind on snow. "And it's not in the cupboards either," I went on. "And I don't think it's anywhere on the counter." I looked around. "The drawers maybe…" The tremor intensified into an itch inside my chest, a sort of light interior tickle. I glanced at the line of open drawers and picked the nearest one. It was full of cookbooks. "It's in here somewhere," I said.

I began to pull the books out one at a time. Out of the corner of my eye, I saw Miss O'Shea's head jerk forward and her mouth fall open, but I paid no attention. I was almost there. It was close at hand. I shook each book over the counter: Joy of Cooking, The Five Roses Cookbook, Kate Aitken's Canadian Cookbook, Fanny Farmer. As I was doing this, I was also dimly aware of noises far away, a clattering on the stairs and voices.

Under the Fanny Farmer was a thick pocket book. *The Well of Loneliness*. Not a cookbook surely with a title like that. I shook it hard, but no ring fell out. I had glimpsed a dark shadow among the pages, so I turned the book over in my hand and let it fall open. It parted in the middle section. A neat cube had been cut into the pages in the centre of the book. The ring was there as I knew it would be, Scotch-taped down inside in its paper container. A paper well, I realized, and for Miss Gatherum, a well of loneliness indeed. How sad. I turned to Miss O'Shea, but she was not in the room.

As I stared at the twinkling thing, it winked back at me with a tiny flick of light. "See, you found me after all," it seemed to say. "I knew you would."

The shimmery feeling in my gut was floating away now, replaced by flat-out panic. I vaguely heard voices and laughter coming from the hall, but my brain was in full spin. I knew what had taken place and it wasn't welcome. I had caught the family disease. The psychic ability to find things. The hereditary ailment that ran through the generations. The so-called *Gift*.

Oh God, I was fey. No way. No bloody way was I going to give in to a life of tea leaves and needy people. It was fine for some creepy cottage in Scotland, but not in Canada. *This is the new world over here*, I said sternly to the rapidly diminishing part of my consciousness. *No weird voices and hocus-pocus for me, thank you very much.*

Out loud, I whispered firmly, "Bugger off."

At that minute, I knew I had to get outside, get away from the noxious ring and the vague feeling of triumph for finding it. I rushed out to the hall, but it was full of women, among them Bubsie. "Janet," she said. "We hear you're helping out. And we are too."

She introduced me to the others, but I could not grasp the names. I recognized Miss Joliette, my old Grade 8 teacher and Miss Treloar who gave private music lessons at people's houses. Old Mrs. Hutchin, my Latin teacher, was there too.

I was grappling with my coat and, at the same time, moving toward the door when I saw Miss O'Shea. Her face looked rosy now and happier. It was as if her life had turned around. I pushed the book into her hands. "It's in here," I said. From the babble around me I overheard the words *Elaine* and *Winnipeg*.

A minute later, I was running down the stairs, my overshoes flapping. I did not stop until I hit the cold winter air.

I told no one about my newly discovered and unwelcome mystical gift. I simply mentioned to my mother that the ring had been found in the apartment as she had foretold. Her reply was a grunt.

The following Friday evening at work in Eaton's, I tried to ask Bubsie a few questions about the Sisterhood, but she was not forthcoming. Like my mother, she gave a sort of grunt. "Huh," she said. "Mary Margaret O'Shea," she sighed, drawling out the name.

"The brains of a moth. But she's our friend so we'll stick by her, I suppose."

She handed me the bottle of lemon oil and set me polishing the varnished counters. "And I'm not going to be a bridesmaid, Janet, if that's what you want to know. And none of our gang is either. I told her to get some of those O'Shea cousins. God knows there's a lot of them. It'll be hard enough to get through the damned wedding, not to mention all the bridal showers they're lining up."

So, there was a happy ending after all. It was a satisfying thought. Miss O'Shea had not changed her mind about getting married. In fact, plans for the wedding were underway. Wonderful news.

I almost mentioned this out loud to Bubsie, but something stopped me. I decided, on balance, it would be better to keep silent.

THE RIGHT THING
by Brenda Fisk

Sprawled across the sidewalk, his entire body shuddered when her boot collided with his face. A smear of red stained the concrete and he made no move to defend himself.

She grimaced and delivered a second vicious kick.

The car behind me honked when the light turned green. I kept my foot on the brake and rolled down my window.

"Hey!" I hollered. "Stop that!"

The woman lined up another strike to the man's skull while her companion stomped his chest.

Vehicles proceeded through the intersection and the driver on my bumper laid on the horn. At the earliest opportunity, he cut around me, middle finger raised where I could see it.

Were they blind, or did they not care? Was it because these were street people? Were they invisible?

Not to me.

~ ~ ~

Choosing integrity over self-interest isn't easy, but three decades ago Deirdre Watts showed me I could do the right thing.

I'd met Deirdre that summer, but I wouldn't exactly call us friends. She was a civilian employee who actually spoke to police summer students like me, and the only person who'd rent her basement cheap. There was something about her I was too young to recognize, only that she seemed an old lady in a younger woman's shell.

Divorced and desperately lonely, the

furrows in her brow and the grim line of her mouth suggested that it might always be so. To fill the void in her heart, she'd turned to her ill-tempered poodle Maximus—and to Jesus.

Her solitary Bible readings were loud enough for me to hear through the floorboards as I shivered downstairs in heavy sweaters and wool socks. Although she only charged me two hundred and fifty bucks a month for access to her basement, her Christian leanings didn't extend as far as allowing me heat. A glass of water left on my kitchen counter overnight froze an inch thick and my scrawny twenty-year-old frame didn't fare much better.

Fresh out of college, I was determined to make it on my own and naïve enough to believe I could survive on part-time minimum wage. That was before the security agency laid me off. Now, a measly half loaf of day-old bread remained until the pantry was bare.

I'd tightened my belt three notches since August, but sheer pride kept me from going home.

A dozen push-ups on threadbare carpet thawed my limbs. Another dozen strained my muscles, but stoked my internal furnace for as many minutes more. With the TV volume low, I switched to sit-ups.

As long as I was silent during the day, Deirdre remained upstairs and ignored me. If I made any noise, she'd reinforce the rules with a shout and the crack of her heel on hardwood.

The chance that she'd put in a good word for me with the police department faded with each mood swing, but there was a stubborn glimmer of hope in my empty belly. It would all be worth it. I was certain.

One particularly cold winter afternoon, I shoveled Deirdre's driveway and was trying to warm up downstairs when she made a rare appearance in my doorway. Her gaze darted around the room as if looking for something to criticize. Had the scraping noises been too loud? I spied a stray sock and nudged it out of sight with my toe.

She focused on me. "Would you like to come up for a hot chocolate—"

"Okay." I was too chilled to possess the self-control necessary for a polite pause.

"—and a Bible discussion?"

I didn't care what had prompted this display of charity, nor did I care that I'd have to listen to her read. I scrambled up the stairs and obediently sat in a kitchen chair. Face above the mug, rising steam warmed my cheeks.

Maxi growled a circle around me and squeezed between his mistress's ankles. One paw poised, the dog stood on his remaining three and glowered.

Too-sweet hot chocolate hit my stomach and the sugar mainlined to my brain. Giddy, I gulped it and burned my tongue.

"So…" I began.

"Don't bother," Deirdre interrupted. "The department isn't hiring."

"Are you—?"

"Yes, I'm sure. There's never been a female Constable, and there never will be. Everyone says so."

"Surely, at some point, they'll have to…" The wooden chair became unbearably hard and I shifted my weight. What had I expected, a sisterhood bond?

"Stop asking," she snapped. "You're embarrassing yourself."

A lump formed in my throat and I choked it down with hot chocolate. The dog had taken a step toward me, nose probing my pant leg. Perhaps there was one ally in this house.

"Here, boy." I reached out a hand and narrowly missed being bitten. Teeth bared above pink gums, Maxi made his alliance known.

The tight line of Deirdre's mouth stretched

180

into a grimace. "He doesn't like strangers."

Neither of us mentioned that I'd lived here for three months and Maxi snapped at me every single day. When would I cease to be a stranger? She took advantage of my awkward silence and read another page before she closed the book with a thump.

Bible clutched to her chest, Deirdre leaned in and fluttered her lashes. "Well, do you notice anything different about me?"

"Uh, your eyes are a little red." Her weird fake eyelashes, like twitchy spiders, were also new.

"No!" Her legs tensed as if she might stand up and whap me with that book. "I got contact lenses." She sat back and fluttered her lashes again.

"Oh." I should have noticed the absence of her thick glasses.

"And I met someone," she blurted, those four words somehow rendering her breathless. "He's from my church and he's picking me up at seven."

I couldn't tell if her eyes were moist from religious fervour, or excitement over the date.

Maxi danced on his hind legs when she got to her feet. She gave him a treat and, miracle of miracles, refilled my mug.

Knowing it would not happen a third time, I savoured this one. Outside, icy wind rattled the frosted window, but in the kitchen my warm belly rumbled in pleasure.

"What do you think of my new outfit?" She tippy-toed a circle, like a child showing off a new dress. This drab grandma skirt and knitted shawl looked as grim as what she'd worn yesterday. Flesh-coloured lace at the hem fluttered when she changed directions for another spin.

I fiddled with the buttons on my shirt. I've always been a terrible liar, and I still had concocted nothing nice to say about her outfit. Now, I consider my inability to lie convincingly one of my redeeming qualities, but as a young adult, I hated that my face broadcast every thought.

Maxi yapped and jumped up, untrimmed nails tearing Deirdre's fancy pantyhose. Did my saccharine-tongued landlady curse under her breath? She stopped mid-spin and fixed him with steely eyes.

Maxi froze.

Like the dog, I stayed perfectly still. He knew her far better than I.

"Max-i-mus!" she shrieked, stomping her heel. "Bad dog! Go on, git!"

A low growl in his throat, Maxi shot me an accusatory glare, and commando-crawled out of sight.

The warmth in my belly congealed into a cold lump, but I wasn't willing to abandon the rest of my hot chocolate. I polished it off, uttered a quick "thank you" and set down the mug, careful not to let it clink.

Stuck in an invisible time warp, Deirdre was still standing in the middle of the kitchen, brows hooded over dark eyes, staring at her torn pantyhose. Her lips moved, but no words came.

I escaped down the stairs, hugging the wall to avoid the sullen dog on his return from purgatory. He curled his lip as he passed.

Safe on the tattered couch, I wrapped my arms around my shoulders and imagined I was warm again. I got on the floor and did twenty, and then I did twenty more. I jogged in place, making sure my socked feet were silent as ninjas. I put on mittens, sank into the cushions and read yesterday's paper. I started back at the Help Wanted section and worked my way to Front Page News. Mitts off for reassembly, I folded and replaced it on the recycle pile.

Tomorrow, I'd eat the last of my bread. With a big fat zero in my bank account, I would be forced to call my parents and admit defeat. Cold seeped through my socks and I tucked my legs under me.

Seven o'clock had passed long ago, but I hadn't heard the doorbell. Had Deirdre gone out to meet her date? I peeked through the window. Her truck was sitting in the driveway, still as death. Its orange electrical cord snaked from the block heater to an outlet by the porch. She wouldn't have walked anywhere in this weather, it had to be forty below with the wind chill.

The phone upstairs rang unanswered and I turned away from the window. My landlady's love life was not my business.

With no more energy for push-ups, I headed to the bedroom for a blanket and stopped in the doorway. Right in the centre of my bed, displayed like an unwrapped present, was a Maximus-sized turd. A salty tear burned my eye. I didn't have the heart to wipe it.

This is how failure felt.

I had scarcely finished scraping poo off my blanket when the dog skittered past me and dove under the bed. How dare he! I reached for the broom.

Crash!

Deirdre was at the door, a handful of stainless cutlery jumbled at her feet. Her eyes were so wide the whites startled me, and an alarm sounded in my head. Did she plan to do me harm? For a second, I wondered if I should join the dog.

"You didn't wash your cup." She jabbed a potato masher at me, teetered and fell against the wall. "You're—" Her shoulders drooped. "I dunno." This was not just cranky night shift mood.

I turned on the light in the hallway. Her lipstick was smudged across her cheek, splotches staining one earlobe Barbie pink, but Barbie didn't wear her skirt sideways. A teetotaler, my landlady couldn't be drunk.

"Deirdre?"

She raised her chin in defiance, pupils like terrifying black holes. "I bought a new outfit," she mumbled, clenching a shaky fist. "You… and your cup."

"Deirdre, you're not making sense. What have you done?"

She dropped her fist and crumpled, legs splayed. "He didn't come." Saliva oozed from the corner of her mouth. "He never…"

That's why there had been no doorbell tonight.

The dog whined.

"Did you take something?"

She curled into a fetal position. "Sleep." Eyes closed, tears clung like morning dew to the eyelash spiders.

"Tell me what you took!" Adrenaline sparked through my body.

"Sleeping pill," she muttered.

I hoisted her sagging body upright. "How many?"

"All of them." Her chin bobbled against her chest. "Wanna die."

"We're going to the hospital right now."

"No," she moaned. "They'll fire me."

She mewled like a kitten when I hauled her upstairs and propped her in a chair. Her body slid bonelessly to the floor.

"He… never… came," she whimpered.

"Where are the keys for your truck?" I searched kitchen drawers and examined an empty prescription bottle on the counter. The drug name was gibberish.

"Don't you dare," she mumbled. "You'll never get hired."

"I'm taking you." My landlady's stink-eye had no effect on me tonight. I dumped the contents of her purse on the table and spread it out. The keys went into my pocket.

Deirdre keeled over, cheek plastered to linoleum. Had she passed out? Died? With my fingertips at her wrist, relief overwhelmed me when blood squished through her veins in a steady rhythm.

I snatched the pill bottle, yanked on my boots and skidded down icy steps. The truck shivered to life and I ran back for her when I was sure it would stay running.

Thirty years later, I can't remember if I carried or dragged her outside, or how long it took to drive on slippery roads. I do remember showing the nurses the pill bottle. Amidst raised eyebrows and whispers, I begged them not to tell.

I remember sitting with Deirdre until she awoke. I held her hair while she vomited into a basin, and cried, and swore, and vomited again. I couldn't stop her from sifting through the mess with her hands in search of her new contact lens.

"It's not lost at all," I told her. "It's right there in your eye."

The nurse shook her head and turned away.

My brain buzzed with a mixture of energy and fatigue. When Deirdre was allowed to sleep, I drove her truck home. This time, Maxi didn't bother coming to bark at me, but he'd made the effort to pee on the couch in my absence. I avoided it and crawled onto the unsoiled end of the mattress. Wrapped in my coat, I slept until the sun rose.

Deirdre uttered not a single word when I picked her up from the hospital. She snatched the keys from the ignition the moment we pulled into the driveway, her dark scowl a warning that she didn't want my help with anything. She stepped over the snow-covered morning paper, tromped inside and slammed the door in my face.

I plugged in the truck, shook off the newspaper and brought it in the house. Emboldened by the reappearance of his mistress, Maxi descended on me in an unprecedented flurry of barking, teeth bared at my ankles. I eased past him to remove my boots.

This time, I took the newspaper straight downstairs, sat on the carpet and spread it open. I nearly cried when I saw the Help

Wanted section.

Now Hiring Constables…

"That's my paper." Deirdre hovered just beyond the doorway. Her voice was an ominous monotone.

I pointed to the ad. "Look!"

"You stole my paper." Maxi appeared behind her, head lowered, eyes on me.

"What?"

"Don't you ever tell anyone what happened." She frowned. "I want you out." The dog retreated when she stomped up the stairs.

I hadn't expected hugs and a big thank you, but this hurt. Was she blaming me, or was she afraid I would blab her secret?

Thirty years ago, I blinked back frustrated tears and phoned my parents. I imagined my dad thoughtfully nodding his head as I told my story. My childhood memories include watching the van's taillights glow outside while he warmed the engine late at night.

He'd be home in a few hours, covered in mud, knuckles scraped from helping someone pull their vehicle out of the bush. In the morning, he'd walk out the door with his lunch pail, like he did every workday.

"Mmm, hmm," Mom said. "I'm glad she's okay." Like Dad, she never ignored anyone in need. They didn't complain, nor did they need to explain. It was just something they did, and they'd passed it on to me.

I wasn't ready to admit defeat, but maybe it was my turn. I needed their help to move out and apply for that job.

Deirdre intervened with malicious gossip and I was relieved when it didn't sway the hiring committee. Perhaps, like Maxi, they knew her far better than I.

That winter, the department did hire their first female officer, but not everyone shared my enthusiasm. At least Deirdre was professional when we worked together, and we never spoke of that night. She eventually married and found her own happiness.

One thing I've learned is that people are unpredictable. Victims reunite with their assailants, fingers intertwined like newlyweds, long before wounds heal. Parents hurt children and children hurt too. People hurt each other. They hurt themselves.

As a police officer, I've been sworn at and threatened, kicked, bitten and spat upon more times than I can count. The trajectory of my career was altered by injury one night. My loss is mitigated by the knowledge that, because of my actions, a child did not lose his mother, and a mother got a second chance.

My dreams are scarred. Years of physical pain are embedded in the lines of my face.

And I don't regret helping a single person.

~ ~ ~

I hit the gas and veered across two lanes to take the next right turn. As soon as my tires scrubbed the curb, I flicked on the emergency flashers. Retired or not, I couldn't ignore a vicious assault on anyone.

"What's happening?" From her seat in the back, my ten-year-old daughter stared at me round-eyed in the rear-view mirror.

"It's okay." I kept my tone calm and even. "No big deal. I'll be right back."

She wasn't buying it. She was always my best helper, but right now she needed to stay put.

I turned and met her eye. "There's someone in trouble and I need to help."

Her brows puckered and she reached for her seat belt. "I want to come."

"Not this time." I held up a finger. "You're safe in the car. I'm locking the doors, okay?"

"Okay."

"I'll be back in a few minutes." I gave her a thumbs up and she watched me hurry down the block. Phone in my hand, I dialed 9-1-1.

I hoped that when she grew up, my daughter would do the same.

IAMBIC HEPTAMETER AND THE ABDUCTION OF MURIEL
by Jack Sheddon

Muriel could feel the late May sun through her cotton blouse as she trimmed the grass around her husband's headstone. She smiled as she worked, occasionally glancing across the rows of headstones to view the lazy waters of the Kaministiqua River and gray granite cliffs of Mount McKay in the background. The grass was rich and green, and the lilac flowers in full bloom bent their branches, making the cemetery an almost cheery place to be spending the afternoon. She nodded to herself, thinking that if you had to be dead and buried, then Thunder Bay was a darn good place for it to happen.

Today was her sixty-eighth birthday and

she pondered life, and where the rest of hers would take her. Talking to herself, she snipped and pulled weeds. She still loved Harvey—well, liked him—and probably always would. Viewing herself as a practical woman, she understood that her age left few options in the way of mate replacement, so made no plans for meeting anyone new. It was just that, for the forty-seven years they had been together, she had hated being called Mrs. Stankowitz.

Dropping the clippers into her cloth tool bag, she decided that it was finally time to do something about that. Using a garden trowel to measure around the base of a terracotta flower pot, she cut circles in the sod and scooped out enough dirt to drop flowers into holes on either side of the headstone.

"I know you hate the smell of marigolds, Dear, but they'll add cheery colour to the site, and I think you'll get used to them. They're a pretty flower, and they were on sale today."

She pushed more dirt into the holes to firm up the plants and watered them from a bottle pulled from the tool bag.

"Harvey, I've reached a decision on what we talked about last week. I know you won't approve, but I've thought about this for a long time and, it being spring and all, I've decided to return to using my maiden name."

She dropped the empty bottle back into the bag and shook her head.

"My whole career, I endured the snickering of my students, the whispers of *Stinky Stankowitz* whenever my back was turned. And I've long ago given up on correcting clerks and bank tellers who misspell and mispronounce my last name, 'No, that's Stankowitz, with an A, not an I.' I'm tired of it, and believe a return to the name of Hennessey will serve me well for what time I have left."

She nodded over at HARVEY, "There, I'm glad that's out of the way. Now we can relax and enjoy the rest of this lovely day."

She dug out a spray bottle of Windex and an old dishcloth and began cleaning the headstone. "I stay busy at home, Dear, but just can't keep up the yard work the way you used to. There are so many things I find difficult now. I manage to get the lawn cut at least once a week, but the lilac bushes are going wild; they're just too tall for me to trim. I think Humphrey from next door is getting a little upset about it. They're growing over the fence into his backyard. He hasn't complained yet, but I saw him taking a look at them. Oh, well, I may have to pay one of the neighbourhood boys to trim them for me."

She stopped wiping and smiled down at the stone. "I've also become involved in a poetry group. I've always loved poetry, the colour and magic in words. I remember trying to teach my Grade 6 kids iambic heptameter—the little monsters hated it—but ahh, the beauty of the *fourteener*.

Shakespeare, Poe, Gordon, they all used it. I've been reading and researching, and did you know that the theme song to Gilligan's Island is a fourteener? Yes, isn't that a surprise? And, you'll love this, remember that silly song from the fifties about the Witch Doctor? You used to sing it when you were puttering in your workshop."

She sat up and grinned, "And that other one, you know, *I've got the joy, joy, joy, joy down in my heart.*" She nodded her head, keeping time with the song. "Remember that one? It was fun."

She paused, smiling shyly, "I'm even dabbling a bit, putting down a few words. I know I'm not very good, but it is exciting, and doing the writing longhand seems to help with the arthritis in my fingers."

Muriel began to hum the song to Gilligan's Island while digging at a stubborn piece of dirt embedded in the Y.

"I've also joined another group." She

stopping singing and took a deep breath. "It's called the Looking Up Society. They believe the earth is being visited by beings from other planets."

"There, I've told you that too." She shrugged and resumed cleaning. "Today seems to be a day for getting things out into the open. I know what you think of the subject—aliens and extraterrestrials—but the people in my new group are friendly, and very sincere about what they're trying to do. You always argued that extraterrestrial beings didn't exist, that anyone who believed in them was either stupid or gullible. I will admit that you did come up with some interesting points against them." She nodded at HARVEY. "Remember the discussions, well, arguments we used to get into over it? I still say that it is the height of arrogance to believe that this planet holds the only life in the Universe."

Muriel scowled and began to speak with a

faked, deep voice, "I'm not saying that we are the only life in existence, Muriel, I really do think the Universe is teeming with life. What I am saying is that on this planet alone billions of species have come into existence, evolved, and gone extinct. And of those species, only one has developed enough intelligence to brew a good cup of tea!"

Muriel smiled and patted the top of the headstone.

"You always loved your tea, Dear."

She got back to wiping at the stone.

"You had an answer for everything, Harvey. When I would point out the many, many cases of alien contact as proof, you could always provide a counterargument."

"Hmph," she began, sliding back into her best Harvey imitation. "Tell me Muriel, why would a race of beings of great intelligence—conquerors of space, defeaters of the limits imposed by the rules of physics and the speed of light—why would such superior beings travel millions of light years to get to Earth, just to abduct a few residents from a trailer park, and then shove probes up their asses. What would they hope to learn?"

Muriel smiled and shook out the dishcloth.

"I never approved of you swearing, Dear, but you did make a good argument on those points. I just chose to believe. And I think I'm a better person for it."

She stood and brushed away the bits of grass that clung to her knees. "Weather permitting, I'll be back next week. I'll tell you all about the meeting of my new group." She gave HARVEY a pat on the top, picked up her bag, and walked away singing about Gilligan.

~ ~ ~

Muriel awoke confused, having difficulty believing she was not still asleep and dreaming. She remembered leaving the meeting of the Looking Up Society and driving the dark country road towards the highway. The confusion came when she thought about the bright lights that appeared over her car, as the engine died and it rolled to a stop. She winced, remembering the high-pitched whine of whatever floated above her vehicle.

She tried to lift her arm, hoping to give herself a pinch in an effort to wake up fully, but her arms and legs wouldn't respond when she tried to move them. She could move her head, open and close her mouth, and her chest rose and fell as she breathed. Through the skin of her back and bottom she could feel the cold, smooth surface she was lying on.

"I'm naked," she said, her voice quivering.

She squinted at the bright lights above her, then lifted her head to scan down her body.

"Oh my God! Somebody shaved me!" She

panicked.

"What is going on?" she asked the brightly lit, but empty room. "Where am I? Why am I like this? Is this a hospital—an operating room? Am I dead?"

From somewhere out of her field of vision she heard a door whoosh open softly, and the skittering sounds of feet approaching. She stared in silent horror as a short being with wrinkled gray skin and large black eyes walked up and stood beside her. It ran an instrument that glowed with blue light over her body, holding it up to show her the strange writings on a screen at its top.

"Who... What?" she tried to ask.

The being made calming motions with its free hand, while holding up the instrument once again for Muriel to see.

"I don't know what that means!"

The gray being wagged its head from side to side, pressed a sequence on the screen, then passed the glowing instrument over

205

Muriel's head and torso. She immediately felt a warming glow settle over her and began to calm down.

"What did you do?" she slurred, having difficulty focusing her eyes. "Whatever it was, I feel really good right now. Woo hoo! I think I want to sing. I'm not very good at it, in fact my husband used to say I had a voice like two seagulls fighting, but I feel a song in me trying to get out. Woo hoo!"

The Gray patted her on the shoulder, then turned and began to walk away.

"I've... got... the... joy, joy, joy, joy, down in my heart. Woo hoo!" Muriel sang-shouted up at the lights. "Down in my heart. Woo hoo! Down in my heart!"

The Gray rushed back to her gurney, waving its thin arms, making a *stop doing that* signal.

Muriel looked up at it, confused. "I guess you don't you like that song." She smiled and shrugged. "I understand. It doesn't quite stay true to the rules of iambic heptameter."

"Oh... you might not know about that. It's a poetry form we have here on Earth." She stopped to swallow, then licked her lips. "My tongue feels fuzzy right now. Do your people write poetry? Have you ever heard of Shakespeare? What about Casey at the Bat? Do your people teach that in whatever passes for grade school where you come from? Why are my eyes making squishy sounds?"

"I've... got... the... joy, joy, joy, joy, down in my heart."

The Gray waved its arms, trying to get Muriel to stop singing.

"Down in my..." Muriel noticed the Gray's frantic waving and stopped. "I guess you don't like music," she said thickly. "What about a poem, then? Something lighthearted that will go good with a numb tongue and squishy eyes. Woo Hoo!" She began to giggle, caught herself and tried to straighten up. "Um... what about Robert Service? My husband, Harvey, used to like his work."

Muriel slipped into her Harvey voice, "The Northern lights have seen queer sights, but the queerest they ever did see was that night on the marge, of Lake Lebarge, I cremated Sam Magee..."

The Gray let out a squeal and clapped its hands over the holes on either side of its head.

"By the way," she said, trying hard to keep her eyes from crossing. "I don't appreciate you shaving me down there." She began to giggle again, "Not while I'm asleep, anyway."

The Gray pulled its hands away from its head and made shushing motions at Muriel.

"Hey... I was just wondering..." Muriel stopped, forgetting what she was about to ask. Focusing hard, she looked over at the Gray and frowned in concentration, "Oh... right. Have I been probed? I don't think I would like that. But... I do wonder... has anyone ever written a piece in heptameter that deals with probing? Maybe I could be the first."

The Gray stared at her.

"I've... got... the... joy, joy, joy, joy..." The Gray clapped its hands over its ear holes and fled the room.

~ ~ ~

At age sixty-eight, on a warm Saturday afternoon near the middle of June, Muriel reached what she believed was another important decision. Talking and nodding, she pruned marigolds and trimmed grass around HARVEY as they discussed life, and where the rest of hers would take her. As a practical woman, she understood that telling people about her abduction, even members of the Looking Up Society, would only open her to ridicule. They would say that it was impossible, that she was just a lonely old woman looking for attention. She wasn't about to start displaying her new shave just to prove herself to any doubters.

"So, the Gray ran out of the room and I blacked out. When I awoke the sun was coming up and I was back in my car, fully dressed. I just didn't feel right, I thought I might have had a stroke, so I drove to the hospital to get checked out." She smiled and gave HARVEY a pat on top. "They thought I'd gone crazy, kept me in for two weeks, Dear. I've only got home on Thursday. That's why I haven't been by to see you."

She gave HARVEY another pat. "How is that for strange, Dear? I know you find this hard to believe. I understand your skepticism, but I want you to keep an open mind, Take things slow and easy. It will be easier for you to digest, if you take it in small bits and bites.

Well, Dear, there are a couple of other things we need to discuss today. First, I've changed my mind over returning to my maiden name. I've decided that remaining Mrs. Stankowitz is probably for the best. I've put up with it for the last forty-seven years, another decade or two will hardly matter."

Muriel hummed and talked as she worked.

"I've been writing a bit, too," she said, smiling shyly. "Nothing noteworthy, just a few lines on life and re-birth, those types of things. I may do a little more research on ballads, they've always appealed to me, and with my interests in heptameter, things should blend together nicely.

"I've got the, hmm, hmm, hmm..."

She dug the bottle of water out of her tool bag to give the marigolds a drink.

"There's something else I want to talk to you about today, and I don't know where to start. It's almost embarrassing." Muriel sighed, a look of determination on her face. "While I was in the hospital, Doctor Riley— he's very good, really young, but very good— well, he gave me the whole treatment, a full exam, blood and urine, that sort of thing. They didn't find anything bad, thank God, but Dr. Riley is confused."

Muriel stopped trimming and bent in closer to HARVEY. "He really is flabbergasted at the results of the tests, says I have the internal workings of a twenty-five-year-old. And..." she leaned in closer to whisper. "I'm three months pregnant."

She stared at the headstone, as if waiting for a reaction.

"You're finally going to be a father, Harvey. After all these years, can you believe it? That's why I've decided against the name change, you see. This way, the baby will be a Stankowitz—our baby." She finalized her statement with a quick nod.

"These marigolds really took well in this soil, Dear." She said, pulling off a withered leaf. "They do add a bit of colour, don't you think?"

She began packing her tools away,

preparing to leave.

"I'm not sure if I'll be visiting every weekend until after the baby is born," she said over to HARVEY. "And I do hope those pesky Grays won't pay me any visits as things get along. But don't worry about me. I'm not frightened of them anymore. If worse comes to worst, a few lines of Sam Magee will set those beings straight. Mrs. Muriel Stankowitz can take care of herself, Dear."

Muriel stood, dusted off her knees and made it three steps away from the graveside before disappearing in a flash of light.

WILD THING
by Maria Morrison

The world has a scent, one that fills the wild places where men rarely tread. When they do, it clings to them, pervading everything artificial, reminding us of what is real.

That was how she smelled as she strolled up to his counter—like something untamed. When he looked up to take her order, he found himself lost in her. In her scent and the brightness of her eyes. The smile which bared her teeth, and the brown of her skin, baked in the sun. There was nothing artificial about her.

His reaction was not lost to her. She laughed to see him so enraptured, not cruelly, more like she was used to such attention. Perhaps she was.

"S-sorry," he stammered, feeling blood rush to his face. "What can I get you?"

Her forest scent—subtly kissed by salt—danced around him, bringing to mind evergreen places and lichen strewn carpets, running rivers and surging tides. It rose above the omnipresent bouquet of coffee and warm pastry. His heart raced and his mouth was dry. It was impossible to ignore.

She didn't seem to notice his discomfort. Her attentions had turned to the chalkboard menu above him. It gave him a chance to observe her in what was clearly not her natural environment. Her long hair had been drawn into a tail that ran down her back, but it was still unruly. Stray hairs floated about her face, catching the sunlight filtering in through the window behind her. Like a halo of fire framing her face. An earthbound angel, clad in flesh.

Her clothes, in contrast, were plain, but she made them perfect. Fading jeans, and a dark jacket pulled over a black T-shirt. He could not see her feet, but he knew somehow that she wore boots. He could see their mud stains in his head.

He almost didn't catch her order. "One coffee, black as night, and, good gods, is that an éclair in the case? One of those. That's it, unless you want my number."

It caught him off-guard. His racing heart drummed a tattoo in his ribcage. This time, she didn't giggle. She simply smiled that wild grin. Her lips revealed canines, he suspected that she could eat a man alive. Her eyes watched him, unwavering, daring him to say yes.

"Uh... I... I ..." His tongue didn't seem to want to work. He had lost control of himself.

She didn't interrupt his stuttering. She simply stood there, waiting patiently. No one was behind her, and she seemed prepared to stay until she had an answer.

"I-I guess?" he finally managed. As soon

as he said it, he wondered what he was thinking! This girl was out of his league. She probably got up at dawn to yoga and run and drink smoothies made from organic grasses. He wasn't prepared for that sort of commitment.

Still, her smile impossibly widened and, as she paid for her items, she drew a pen seemingly out of the air and waited for her receipt. Leaning over, she scribbled her number on it before sliding it back over the counter.

"It's a landline," she warned him, as he pushed her coffee and treat back across the counter. She simply picked the éclair up off the white plate, taking a bite right there. The custard inside oozed from the back, but she didn't seem to care. Her eyes rolled up into her head in ecstasy, as though she had never encountered such flavours. "I haven't quite made it to the twenty-first century," she said nonchalantly, no apology in her voice.

He laughed awkwardly, wishing he could say something clever. Instead, he picked up the receipt. Above the number she had written a name: *Terra*. It seemed fitting. When he looked up to thank her, he found her gone. Only her scent remained: fresh earth, sky and a hint of the sea. Ageless.

The rest of the day felt like a dream, unreal, as though he now swam through water. His world had become illusory in her wake, as though she had revealed something to him.

When it came time to leave, his boss asked him if he were well. She told him to take the next day off. He accepted faintly, and stepped out into the town.

Above, the sky had turned a deep velvet blue. Already stars were peering through the twilit expanse, only the brightest breaking through the light pollution. He could smell cooling asphalt, acrid engine exhaust and pizza. Her scent had long since faded, drowned out by those of an artificial world. He'd never realized how sharp it all was.

Sidling into his car, he drew the paper from his pocket and stared at it. Her scrawl was as wild as her hair—barely contained to the paper. He wondered if calling her now would make him creepy. Or desperate seeming.

For an eternity he sat there in indecision, the paper in one hand, his cellphone in the other. Twice he put her number in, twice he deleted it. He had never been this nervous before with women, then again, he had never been the one approached. Usually, he was the one initiating. Everything about her had been disarming, and he wasn't sure he liked that.

What he did know was that he liked *her*. Liked her smile, despite how untamed it was. Liked her clothes, despite how plain they were in comparison. Liked her boldness, and her smell. He wanted to know what those eyes had seen.

Typing in the number a third time, he took a deep breath and hit the green button. It rang. Once, twice, three times—then her voice answered. "Hello?"

"Hi," he said, unsure of what to say. "You, ah, you gave me your number today, at-at the bistro? I just got off work and I have tomorrow off, so maybe you'd like to get together?"

There was nothing unsure about her answer. "Yes! Absolutely. I was just getting ready to head out, want to come along? If you don't work you can sleep in tomorrow! Are you still at work? I can come pick you up!"

He was taken aback. "Out? Now?"

"Yeah! The stars are out, perfect night! You probably can't see them well in town." She sounded excited.

"O-okay. Yeah, I'm in the parking lot."

"Cool beans! I'll see you in ten!" Then she was gone.

220

He stared at the phone, wondering what he had just done. It was night, time to sleep. Feeling flustered, he gathered his coat around himself and stepped out of the vehicle, locking it. Waiting.

It took her six minutes to arrive.

She was dressed just as she had been this morning. He climbed into her pickup truck, mud splattered on the outside, but clean within. She was grinning behind the wheel, a telescope laying in the space beside her. She moved it closer to herself as he seated himself. Her wild scent washed over him, kissing him full on the mouth.

For the first time since she had left, he felt real again. "You're going to love this," she promised, pushing the truck into gear. It slid onto the road smoothly.

Onwards they drove, a peaceful silence between them. She continued smiling, her hair blowing in the wind as she cranked the window down. Away from the town they drove, away from the lights and the artificial world, towards a new place alien to him.

Pulling onto a side road, the forest surrounded them. He didn't know where they were going, but he no longer cared. As he drank in the smell of the world, the *real* world, he knew it didn't matter. She had ensnared him, and awoken him to something new. There was no going back, not as the heavens opened above him into glory, and a wild angel sat at the wheel.

Together, they drove into the night.

"So how long have you lived in the Valley?" she asked, pushing the truck into gear as they slipped up the edge of the tall hills which overlooked his home, following some secret road.

"A-a few years," he stuttered, looking out at the dark world beyond his window. The only lights were the headlights of the truck, and he wasn't sure he could navigate his way back if he tried. His heart hammered in his chest, and his hand steadied the telescope which lay between them. It jumped and jittered like something living as the terrain beneath the tires gave way to what sounded like gravel or dirt. "You?" He knew nothing more of this woman than her name and her coffee order.

"All my life," she said cheerfully. "Born and bred, Valley strong." She thumped a fist twice between her breasts, and howled. He laughed despite himself, and she joined him. It was a wonderful sound.

"So, where are we going, exactly?" he ventured, beginning to feel comfortable again.

"Don't worry, I'm not going to kill you," she joked, a glint in her eye. "We're going to where we can see the stars. Gotta get above the light pollution, ya know? There's a clear cut up this way. Bit of a bumpy ride and a total shame, but my Gods, the stars!"

Thoughts of bears, seen rambling on nearby roads and promptly published on

223

Facebook, filled his mind immediately. Flashbacks of radio reports of coyote sightings—and even attacks— the year he had come here, drawn by a college education which hadn't quite panned out. He nervously confessed his thoughts, glancing at the darkness which flew around them. She grinned mischievously, "Oh, they won't be interested in this. Bears aren't known to be great astronomers."

She took a sudden and unexpected turn, moving off the dirt road, and onto something which barely qualified to be called such a thing. A few ruts, worked into a greening line leading straight into the forest. The vehicle bucked and rattled beneath them, protesting their journey, but she only leaned an arm out the window, patting it as one might a horse. "You got this, old girl. We're almost there."

Weird shapes and dark voids loomed around them, and above the sky had vanished entirely. They flew through a tunnel and emerged in another world.

He had never imagined a sky like this.

Shifting down, she rolled the truck to a stop and killed the lights, sitting in the darkness, seeming to drink it all in. "Under your seat is a Maglite," she said, unbuckling her belt and picking up the telescope, "grab it, we're gonna need it."

Blindly, he reached beneath the seat, his hand encountering something large and rubbery. Pulling it out, he found it to be a surprisingly heavy flashlight the size and relative shape of a brick. He fumbled with his belt as Terra opened her door. The earthy bouquet of old wood and new growth hit him, and he swiftly followed her into the unknown.

Without the roof of the truck overhead, he felt as though he could fall into the sky. Above them swirled a bridge of stars spanning one horizon to the other, colours he had never imagined held within their depths. As he stood in the darkness, he felt humbled by the heavens. At the same moment, his skin crawled, remembering that in this place he was the trespasser. Though she had made light of his concerns, he could feel dangerous creatures all around him.

"Shine that light over here!" she called from somewhere in front of the truck. He looked down at his hand, feeling with his fingers for something which might have been a power switch, and when he did, a strong beam shot from the mirrored surface, illuminating a line of deadwood. Terra was already bravely striding through it, seemingly unaware of the dangers. "C'mon," she urged, beckoning him. He hurried to follow, picking his way through the difficult terrain. After what felt like an eternity, she sank to her knees, eyes gazing towards the endless expanse.

Expertly, she dropped the tripod's legs and aimed the body of the telescope to the sky. She peered through one end, a picture of near stillness. Seated before the altar of the

226

cosmos, only a patient hand moved, slowly turning dials he didn't understand. "Turn off the light," she said. Hesitantly, he did.

The sounds of the night rose around them as they sat there: the hum of insects as they swirled around unseen, the peeping of the tiny wood frogs as they sang to one another, and the mysterious cries of things he could not identify. Without the light, the Milky Way once more spun dizzily above, reminding him of how immense the world truly was.

"You okay back there?"

Her voice was comforting, no hint of jest in it. "Y-yeah," he said, not at all feeling confident. What was he doing out here?

"I think I have it, want to see?"

He found he did. Without the light, his eyes had begun to adjust and he could make out her form and the long tube of the scope. Trusting her path, he stepped forward, and came to kneel carefully beside her. She shuffled away from the instrument, and let him place one eye upon the viewer.

There, brightly lit by the sun, was an orb, hanging in the heavens. It swirled with an iridescent light, unlike any he had ever seen on earth. Taking his eye from the scope he looked up, wondering what heavenly body she had set her focus upon. Her hand closed on his shoulder and with the other she pointed towards one bright star. Brighter than any of the others.

"It's Venus," she said. "Normally Sirius or Polaris are brighter, but she's really close to us right now. It makes her easy to spot and easier to see!" Her excitement was clear, and he wished he could see her smile.

Looking upon the planet's brightness, he again moved his head to look upon its beauty. "That's amazing!" He relinquished the scope to her, and watched as she regarded the heavens again. She didn't peer back into it, instead she turned her attention to him.

Adrenaline rushed through him, and he felt her draw closer. Shoulder to shoulder, they sat in awed silence. Her hand found his, and she sighed. "Thanks for coming along. I'll be honest, I've never done anything like this before." Her own confession surprised him, "Usually, I come alone."

"Up here?"

He felt her rather than saw her nod, a subtle motion that moved through her.

"Doesn't it frighten you?"

"Sometimes," she said. "It's my chance to be brave. Most things are frightened of us, though. The light and the truck scare them away. It's worth it to be able to see it all."

He looked back at the truck, a dark hulk sitting at the edge of the clearing. "It is," he finally agreed. "This was definitely worth the time." Her arm crept about his shoulder, and her lips brushed his cheek. Her breath, smelling of something sweet, caressed his skin. He shuddered deliciously, lightning coursing in his veins.

"Then we'll do this again," she promised, her hand was now pulling him towards the truck. "Want to spot the constellations? I have a blanket in the bed of the truck!"

All his life he had gazed at the stars, now he realized he'd never seen a quarter of them. He desperately sought the North Star, hoping to find his bearings. By the time he found it, she had spread the blanket along the back and was lying down upon it, face towards the open sky. The blanket smelled of hay and wood sap.

Almost immediately, her hand began tracing the invisible lines of the sky, showing him how to spot the tiny pattern which made up Orion's belt, and the curving line of Draco as it slid through the Dippers. One hand remained firmly in his, tightening every time he managed to discover the pictures hidden in the heavens.

He didn't know how long they lay there,

surrounded by the majesty of nature and the company of each other, but when they did once again rise, his body complained of the movement. She laughed at him gently and rolled up the blanket, glancing at her watch. The old-school Timex lit up with a touch. "It's almost two," she announced. "Do you want me to drive you home, or would you rather get your car at the Bistro?"

The time surprised him. He had never been out so late. He wasn't even tired as they worked to pack up the telescope. Venus had long moved out of its sights. "I'm good to drive," he promised. "The Bistro would be great, thank you."

Piling back in, she again turned on the headlights and maneuvered out of the lot, back onto the trail which had led them here. They said very little as they drove along, eventually finding the pavement once more. It felt like he was re-emerging after a long absence, the street lights almost alien after the deepest dark of the wood. Baptized by that darkness, he watched it all slip by. Below them as they drove, the lights of the Valley stretched out, the town clear as it curved along the river. Beyond it, the other mountain rolled with equal grace. Above it all, a muted sky swirled, its mysteries lost in the racket of lights.

When they rolled into the parking lot, he was loath to return. To that world of nine-to-five where everything was artificial. He opened his door, and paused.

"Terra," he said, remembering her words about fear. He was plenty afraid now.

"Yes?"

"I want to see you again."

He could see her smile in his mind's eye. "I'd like that," she said.

Before he could lose his nerve, he turned and planted a kiss onto her lips. She received it as he had hoped, with a gentle welcoming. She tasted of blackberries and heavy cream, tinged with sugar and spruce gum. Her scent surrounded him as never before, and he let it fill him.

When it ended, she seemed breathless, and her smile softened. "Tomorrow night, then?"

"Will Venus be out?"

"I'm sure we can find her," she said, "If not, there's a whole universe to explore."

He slid out of the cab, smiling back. No longer afraid. "Tomorrow then," he promised, knowing that they'd have many more tomorrows to explore together. He was ready. Forget about Venus—he had found his North Star.

THE POWDERMAN
by Michael Foy

"We follow blast protocol here, Will. *Warning Signal. Blast Signal. All Clear.* No one gets killed that way. So, get out there and give it ten long pulls. You should be good at that by now," Jerry says, pushing the column shifter into park.

He grabs the two-way radio, says, "All good down here. Green light. Starting blast protocol," and places the handheld back on its hanger.

"10-4," comes the response.

"Go, Will, go, go," Jerry tells me.

Some say you work better when someone watches you. I say horseshit. What I get is even more likely to screw things up, especially when it's Jerry LaDouceur staring over my shoulder. He tells people to call him Deuce, but no one does, and behind his back the guys call him Douche—because you can't make up your own nickname.

Jerry's our mechanic, the Pitt River Quarry know-it-all. He's short, with a shaved head and a neck bigger than my thigh. He's like a human plug, all thick and round and ready to stop things up. His arms, like ham hocks, rest on the truck's steering wheel. He wears his grease on his fingers and knuckles, and has it smeared across his face like a quarterback's eye black. He's always holding a cigarette, with the smoke winding around his head like he smoulders, ready to ignite.

Competition for mine resources happens above and below ground—sure, there's the granite, but it's more than that. Jerry and Daniels fight for the better job, more money, and Daniels' wife Maria. They're mining for hatred. Once, Jerry choked Daniels out for sharpening drill bits. Daniels is local 168—

wrong union, wrong job, and he was doing it in front of the wrong guy. Jerry told him to turn off the sharpener, twice, but Daniels just kept on givin' 'er, thought he could ignore him. Jerry reached up, put him in a half nelson, and dragged him from the machine. "Bud," Jerry whispered in his ear, "that is my fucking livelihood."

Daniels, his face tomato-red, tugged at Jerry's forearm, even tapped at it with the palm of his hand—but Jerry wouldn't let up, and Daniels went limp. His steel toe boots fell together pigeon-toed before skidding over a length of chain and a triangular piece of scrap metal.

Jerry laid him out on the pea gravel like he was laying down one of his kids for an afternoon nap, tossing his yellow hardhat on the ground beside him. "He'll wake up in a minute or so," he said, "with a brand new take on the division of labour."

All that happened two weeks ago. When

things go wrong at the quarry, you can't exactly call up the labour relations board and file a complaint.

Right now, I'm a nothing. I get the crap jobs, and someone has to watch and give me all the advice I can handle: 'No, no, no that goes there. Never, never start here, Will. Make sure that you're standing at least this far back before you put the power on. Why would you do that? Were you even listening to what I said?' But still, I wonder who watches the guys at the top.

In three weeks, I start training for my blasting ticket. Daniels is the powderman now, our explosives expert, but he's taking off for Alberta and the almighty oil fields. At lunch we hear all about it.

"They gotta drill those wells. Am I right, boys? We should all go." He rubbed his thumb across his fingertips. "That's where the money is."

"It's a lateral move, Daniels, a lateral

move," Jerry said. "And a total waste of time."

"Ya, well fuck you, Jerry. None of this matters to you anyways, all you do is fix our shit when we break it. Any jackoff can do that. But if I don't show up for work tomorrow, and there's no blast, you're sent home. You're a fucking lateral move Jerry, your whole life is one big lateral move."

I listened to them argue and ate my ravioli, swiping a slice of buttered bread along the lid of the can for that last smear of thick red sauce. I washed it all down with a half carton of Tropicana orange juice, buried my hand in a bag of sunflower seeds, filled one cheek, walked over to the front step of the dry, sat down and spat out shells.

There was a huge truck tire outside the dry turned on its side, the center filled with black earth and a half dozen tomatoes growing all thick and green. Daniels has a green thumb, and the Beefeaters are red and plump, ready to be eaten. When you work at an open pit mine it's easy to imagine some place better, and whenever I had a moment, that's what I did. And lately, I looked at the guys I worked with—will that be me one day? They're worn out, expired, like an old singer in a rock band. For my backup, I applied to teacher's college. A two-year program. The classes start in the fall. The money isn't great, but how much money do you really need? Besides, summers off, that's gotta be worth somethin'. The academic counsellor said, "It's a chance to work with tomorrow."

My older brother always said I would make a good teacher.

"Don't get stuck at the mine, Will. It grinds away at you, till there's nothin' holding you up but the powder."

"Yeah, but I like construction," I told him. "At the end of the day I can look back and see what I've done. The bags lifted, holes dug, and boulders blasted. The crushed rock at the end of each conveyor is used for roads, dock pilings, and ballast. I helped put it there."

After I'd said that, I realized how stupid it sounded, because you could put just about anything that anyone does in that sentence and act all proud—like you're doing your piece for the greater good—but how do you really know? Is laying a sheet of asphalt over the ground a good thing? Is covering the planet in pavement? The truth is, I'm not sure what I wanna do.

I fumble with the door handle before I get out of the pickup and into the summer heat. It's August and my T-shirt and jeans are brittle under a layer of sweat and caked-on dust. Standing here at the powder magazine, I can see the Pitt River down below, winding its way through fields of potatoes and corn and into Pitt Lake, resting at the base of Thompson Mountain. It's Friday, and at shift's end I'll swim on my back in those blue-gray waters. I'll get the Irish Spring and the bottle of Head & Shoulders from the glove box, and I'll lather off that layer of dust, I'll loosen the gravel in my hair. I pull the air horn over and over: *seven-eight-nine-ten, Warning Signal*, because it gets me closer to jumping into that water.

This is Daniels' last blast. If I make powderman, it means going up the pay scale, and then bring on the overtime. When you run the blast, you're important. They need you. No more boulder hopping carrying a jackhammer, no more hoofin' bags of ANFO, because you're King Shit on Shit Mountain. No one screws with the powderman; without him, nothing happens. No boulders to feed the crusher, no oversize to re-pile and blow again. All the front end loaders, the dumpers, parked—a giant row of unused Tonka toys. The two scows sit empty too, resting high up on the water, bumping the pilings. Without the powderman the Quarry stops dead.

When it goes, this blast will blow the face

clean off bench three, but I know it's the faces in upper management that Daniels wants changed. He's fed up. He has two boys at home, aged six and eight. Maria is expecting and she's getting on his case about how little money's coming in.

"Maria talks about money like its water shootin' up from the ground and I just need to catch it in a bucket." Daniels said. "She's expecting, alright—expecting me to become a millionaire."

Money's only part of the problem. Maria's had it with Daniels and his drinking, and the coke. With each gram coming in at $100, he can't continue on this slippery slope. Eventually, he'll go down. He spends most of his time at the Gilnetter drinking beer and snorting his wages in a rolled-up twenty. It's like he's holed up in an army bunker, surrounded by barbed wire and deep trenches, and his wife and kids are the enemy. He just needed to roll out a table map, hold each corner down with a glass of beer, and explain his plan of attack. You won't get me outta here alive.

After a couple of trips into the Gilnetter bathroom, Daniels came to life with all the energy and optimism of a caged man. He knew he could talk here. He was safe at the pub. He told us that the block of blue granite would soon run dry and we'd all be collecting UI. He was afraid of something, but nothing we could see. According to Daniels you had to have a Plan D, a way out of a place that had completely caved in. But we knew that granite was good for another half-century.

Last Saturday, Jerry came to the Newton Inn at two in the afternoon. Daniels and I had been drinking beer, playing pool, and watching the dancers spin on the pole for a couple hours. Daniels was half in the bag when Jerry showed up. Jerry stared at the ground as he walked in from the too-bright sunshine. His brow was furrowed. It created this long ripple of skin on his forehead, like he was trying to sprout horns. Jerry circled the pool table and grabbed a handful of Daniels' shirt, knocking a pack of Craven A's to the floor.

"Your red Chevelle's in the goddamn parking lot," Jerry said, pushing and pulling Daniels in time with the words—you could hear Daniels' collar tear. "Your two boys sittin' out there in the back seat. It's summer, for Christ's sake!"

Daniels made an arm circle and came down hard with his elbow on Jerry's forearm, and broke his grip. "Whatever Douche, if I'm losing, let me lose," Daniels said. "That's what I came here for." He stepped on his pack of cigarettes on his way back to the table, lined up his shot and struck the cue ball, sending the balls clacking all over, but nothing dropped. His stretched shirt collar hung low from his neck, like a slackened noose, and revealed patches of inflamed skin on his collarbone.

"You gonna get out there or what?" Jerry asked.

The kids are Maria's insurance policy. Daniels has to take the boys on any weekend trips from the house, so she can be sure of a sober return. So much for that.

But two weekends ago, it was Jerry who was too drunk to drive home, and the bartender asked me to give him a lift. When we turned on to the King George, Jerry let it all spill, even broke down crying, said he loved Maria and she had a right to be happy. She told Jerry she's ready to walk. She wants a family again.

With Daniels back at the table and into his game I approached Jerry. "Where were you all afternoon? Shouldn't you be thanking Daniels for getting the kids outta the house?"

Jerry turned to face me, "Pissing with the big dogs now, eh Will? Worry about yourself, this doesn't concern you." He scratched the top of his head, the skin streaked with nail marks.

That was when Jonah, Daniels' eight-year-old son walked right into the bar, all red-faced and sweaty. His brown head of hair reached an inch above the green felt on the pool table. He lifted his face up to look at Jerry. "Can you please tell my Dad that Jason got sick in the back seat of the car; he's not feeling too well."

Jonah turned and stared at the lady on stage with his mouth half-open.

Daniels left after that.

~ ~ ~

For this blast, Daniels had wanted all the holes filled with an eight-inch collar.

"When I stand next to any hole I should see ANFO at the top, and not just those holes furthest from the face. You hear me? All the holes."

I knew it meant overspray, boulders—breadbox-sized and floating through the air. Once airborne they would reach the weigh scale trailer. Guaranteed. And that's where the big wigs are having their annual production meeting—one Audi, two Beamers, a Merc, and a chromed-out F-250 towing a trailer with two blue and red Sea-Doos—all parked way down below bench three and within range. They bought the things we couldn't.

After last year's meeting, I had to rinse the dust from their cars with a garden hose. There'd be no rinsing today. The way Daniels has this blast set up, they'll need a front end loader to get at their cars.

"No raise in three years, means no fucking ride home," Daniels said. "Walk a mile in my shoes, boys."

The sun lit up his curly blonde hair and his sun-flecked skin. He wore a T-shirt that read:

Based on a True Story. He smiled, and when he did you saw all of his teeth and it made you wanna smile too, no matter what he was sayin'.

"Better to burn bright and hard than fade out!" Daniels yelled.

"Whoa D-man," I said. "The less I know, the better."

Walking the air-tracks along the top edge of that cliff face, it took us two weeks to drill ninety holes forty feet deep, imbed blasting caps in the gel sticks and drop 'em down, without letting go of the orange cord. Then we filled each hole with ANFO and topped it off with sand and gravel. After that, we tied all the lines together like the grid system on an archaeological dig. These past two weeks, while Daniels was planning a way out, I was planning a way in. He wanted to make a statement, his swan blast. And I'm in on it, whether I like it or not. And now, Daniels is crouched down, waiting to plunge the handle on the shot exploder. Zing. And send 500 volts travelling the line, triggering a blast that will pulverize the granite cliff face.

"Okay, Will. One minute of short pulls."

I pull the chain on the air horn in one-second bursts: *fifty-seven, fifty-eight, fifty-nine, sixty. Blast Signal.*

I see the dust cloud before the car. It's Maria, driving the red Chevelle and tearing up the gravel. She's done it before, swinging the car into the parking lot, ignoring the heavy machinery and other dangers. She flies past and hits the first bench going about fifty kilometres. Her car zigzags up the switchbacks like a spark chasing the fuse. She reaches bench two before I even make it back to the cab.

"That's Maria with the kids in the back!"

"Jesus," Jerry says starting the truck. "Get on the two-way!"

I grab the handheld and press the call button. "Daniels! Daniels! Stop!

Stop the blast!" I listen. Nothing.

Earlier in the day I peeled the coil of line off for the shot exploder, so I know Daniels is about 100 yards back from the blast site, and there is no way he can see Maria flying up that gravel road. No way. Jerry was supposed to secure the swing gate at the mine entrance. No visitors allowed.

If you've ever watched a blast detonate, you know that you can see it a fraction of a second before you hear it. The farther away, the greater the lapse between the movement and the sound reaching your ears. It's a brief look into the future, a stutter in real time.

Jerry and I are on the gravel road and starting our ascent to bench three, Jerry is hammering away on the horn, but all we see is the explosion, the expansion of that peninsula of rock up and out, marked by little grey and black plumes of dust and smoke, like handfuls of chalk powder thrown into the air.

Boom. A thunderous rumble pulses through everything and creates a giant dust cloud that moves slowly toward us, so thick you can't see your hand in front of your face. Jerry hits the brakes and everything slows. The dust cloud hides the falling rock, pieces of it land at different times like the first drops before heavy rain. Some stones hit the ground, others rat-a-tat-tat off the hood of the truck. It lasts for a minute, until all the rock has fallen from above, and we hear nothing. Not even a bird or a scream. And we can't change any of it. No stop, no rewind, on/off, quit, or restart. And Maria and her two kids sure as hell couldn't stop it either. They're buried up there.

~ ~ ~

I look out at my Grade 7 class, just back from lunch and reading silently, their faces lit up from the light reflecting off the pages of their books. Except for Stephano, who's asleep and snoring, the school is quiet.

FAMILY TIES
by Linda White

The Ribstone Creek, a narrow waterway, carves its way through steep, wooded hills near the border between Alberta and Saskatchewan. The Creator reached down and pushed the land into a deep crevice and then planted stands of spruce trees and trembling aspen on the rugged terrain. Cattle share grazing with mule deer, moose and elk. The land holds its own close.

Gerda hadn't slept well. Troubled dreams of Geoff, her sister's son, haunted her. Elsa, his mother, was dead. She died without satisfying her family obligation; instead she'd taken the Baby Geoff and run off. Geoff, now grown, with no idea what he owed, would soon find out. Gerda took her coffee and looked out the window at the creek valley.

"Gonna be nice," said Hank. Gerda and her husband were used to the way the pink dawn spilled over the horizon and painted the hollows and dips subtle gold and rose. Today hoar frost glittered in the early light and furred the branches of the trees.

Gerda made a wifely sound that meant she heard him. She was thinking she should go to town. More and more, she sought the company of other people who provided the warmth her taciturn Hank couldn't.

"If Geoff doesn't call, I'll go to town today."

The phone rang and Gerda answered. She listened, saying little. Hank took the last of the coffee from the carafe.

"That Geoff?" he asked when Gerda ended the call.

Gerda nodded and collapsed onto a kitchen chair. "Hank, I don't think we should do this."

"It's our turn."

Gerda's mouth tightened. "Why? Will it really protect us from them?"

"It's our duty. The boy doesn't have to know."

"He's got some crazy idea of searching the creek for Sasquatch," said Gerda.

Hank snorted. "I'll tell the others," he said.

~ ~ ~

Geoff turned down the lane and stopped the car. He recognized the house from his mother's pictures. Trees had grown to overhang the second story and there was new siding. Huge spruce trees sidled up to the barn.

In family snapshots, Uncle Hank glared like some fire-and-brimstone Biblical prophet. Aunt Gerda stood stiff and serious. This visit could be a mistake, but finding a Sasquatch would be the news story to boost his stalled career. He could handle his odd relatives for that long.

Geoff released the car's brakes and continued up the lane. Two big dogs bounded out to meet him. They circled, barking and jumping. Geoff shut the engine off, but was nervous about getting out. The dogs stopped close to the car and stood panting.

Aunt Gerda opened the front door. Her hair was grey and she looked shriveled. Hank brushed past her and walked over to the car.

Yanking its door open, he said, "What are you waiting for, boy?"

Geoff reddened.

"Bowser, Skippy. Go." The dogs backed off, tails still wagging.

Aunt Gerda hovered in the background by the dogs. "Come in, Geoff," she said. "Bring your bags."

Inside, Geoff put his suitcase down and hung his coat on the peg his aunt indicated.

He left his boots on the mat near the door. Gerda reached out her arms to him and they shared an awkward embrace. Geoff could feel the bones just beneath her skin, poking out knob-like at her elbows and knees. As she hugged him, he felt embarrassed at his own softness.

The kitchen smelled of roast chicken and dressing. On the stove, a large pot of potatoes boiled. An apple pie cooled on the counter. Geoff inhaled. His mother had cooked like this.

"Everything smells great," said Geoff.

Gerda nodded. "I made all of your mother's favourites.

Geoff opened his suitcase and produced a bottle of Shiraz. Gerda thanked him and set it on the counter beside the pie. If the wine loosened Uncle Hank up, Geoff would ask him to help search for Big Foot.

Simple food never tasted so good. Aunt Gerda insisted on cleaning up the dishes herself. "Finish your wine in the den with your uncle," she said. "There's a hockey game."

Geoff followed Hank to the den. "Might as well finish this," he said, pouring the last of the wine into his Uncle's glass.

Hank turned on the TV. News from the local channel involved a strange brew of human interest, area weather and international events. Geoff waited until a long report on the Middle East began and he could see his uncle's interest stray. Hank was a practical man and he didn't have much interest in conflicts on the other side of the world, in places he'd never see.

"Uncle Hank," Geoff began. "My mom told me about the times when everyone went down to the creek to swim."

Hank grunted. "By the beaver dam."

"Did you ever see the tracks?"

His uncle straightened. "What tracks?"

"You know. The Sasquatch tracks."

Hank shrugged.

"You do remember?" Geoff persisted. "Aunt Gerda used to leave them potato salad and fried chicken."

"It's not for me to say." Hank turned back to the TV and feigned interest in the latest car bombing.

"I'm in a bind, Uncle Hank. If you could help me, it would mean a lot."

"What do you want? Spit it out, boy." Hank glowered.

"I lost my job at the paper, so I'm freelancing." Geoff paused. Uncle Hank was a life-long farmer and, to him, work that wasn't at the end of a tool and back-breaking wasn't real work.

"I'm writing articles on spec. I write something and then I send it out and try to sell it."

Uncle Hank grunted. "Sounds iffy to me."

"It's like farming, Uncle Hank. The article is my crop and sometimes it doesn't pay. The crop is hailed out or there's drought. My stories are crops and I tend them like you tend the land. A Sasquatch story could make my reputation." Geoff stopped.

Hank switched the TV channel and the announcers for the hockey game began their pre-game analysis. Geoff held his breath. At the commercial break, Hank turned to him.

"What do you want from me?"

"I need a picture of Big Foot and people to interview. The story could go national, maybe international."

"You want to hunt for Big Foot?" asked Hank.

"Yes," said Geoff. "I know it sounds..." his voice trailed off.

"You sure about this?"

"I'm sure. You won't be sorry, Uncle Hank."

"I'll call the neighbours after the first period." Hank went back to staring at the TV.

The next morning Uncle Hank was up by six o'clock and had the chores done by nine.

260

Three pick-ups rolled into the yard at 9:10. The neighbour men came and had coffee while Gerda made Hank and Geoff sandwiches.

"You Elsa's boy?" asked one. "You must favour your father."

Geoff shrugged.

"I brought the extra skis," said another. "You do ski?"

Geoff nodded. He'd been on cross-country skis once, but the men were all over fifty years old. How fast could four aged men be?

As they put on their skis, Geoff began composing the article in his head. Descriptions of the men, easy. The creek valley was perfect—a pristine wilderness in a rustic community. Discovering Sasquatch in the Ribstone Creek valley would be gold. Everyone thought they were confined to the temperate rainforests of BC and Oregon.

"Ready?" Uncle Hank pushed away from the deck and onto the trail down to the creek.

Geoff lurched into line last.

It wasn't cold, minus ten degrees Celsius, but the men's breath left vapour trails in the crisp air. The snow squeaked under their skis. The path was rough with protruding shrubs and grass that pulled at their feet. Geoff panted. His legs felt wooden and his arms ached. None of the old men was affected. I'll get a second wind, he thought.

The second wind was the breeze that picked up. On exposed slopes and open areas, it snatched at Geoff's breath. Uncle Hank called a coffee break at last. They gathered and, removing their skis, sat in a sheltered hollow under the sweep of a huge fir tree. Hot coffee from a stainless-steel thermos was passed around. Geoff burned his tongue, but he didn't care.

Uncle Hank reviewed their plan; the men would meet on the creek bottom below Hank's house when it got dark. Aunt Gerda and the other women would ride down on

ATVs and they'd have a bonfire and cookout.

They divided the land around the creek into search areas and Geoff was assigned to the steep country on the other side of the creek. Were they testing him or were they giving him the best chance at sighting a Sasquatch?

Uncle Hank stood up and said, "Time's wasting. Be back by sunset."

Geoff skimmed along on the smooth surface of the creek and, as he warmed up, began to enjoy himself. The air was spicy with spruce needles, the sun sparkled on the snow and chickadees chirped in the willows.

Around a bend, a beaver dam formed a pond. The rest of the creek continued six feet below. Geoff swore and turned back.

He re-traced his route and watched for a way up to the higher ground. Then he could follow the creek, but avoid the beaver dams.

Had his uncle set him up to fail?

"I'll show you." Geoff skied with renewed

determination. After a few minutes, he saw a trail leading to the top of the bank.

Geoff removed his skis to push them up the trail first. His camera was in his backpack and he wanted his hands free to keep it safe. He pulled himself up using the sturdy willows growing on the steep bank.

Ten minutes later, Geoff flopped to the ground above the creek. Sweat dripped from under the edge of his toque and his cheeks felt fiery in the brisk air. He rested for a couple of minutes, then struggled to his feet and put his skis back on.

The farther he skied, the wilder the land got. Rugged on either side of the creek rose to meet the clear blue sky. There were no signs of human settlement and it was like he had stepped back through the curtain of time.

Geoff scanned for evidence of Big Foot: tufts of hair, broken limbs on trees, depressions in the snow. He envisioned the headline. *On the Trail of Bigfoot in Eastern*

Alberta, exclusive by Geoff Purdy. If he didn't get a picture of the Sasquatch, he could still put a positive spin on his adventure and get an article out of it.

He pushed forward with ideas spilling into his mind. Without warning, the ground disappeared from under his skis. Jeff sailed into the air and landed hard in the shrubs below.

"Ahhh......" Air burst from his lungs, cutting his scream short. He gasped and struggled for breath. His right ski nestled against his ear and his ankle hurt like hell.

Slowly Geoff raised his head. The ankle looked okay, but felt awful. Sprained or broken. He struggled to sit up and jerked his backpack around so he could check his camera. He found it and pulled it out. Then he got his phone to call Aunt Gerda. She'd send help.

Geoff punched in his Aunt's number and the *no service* signal appeared. Above him, bare branches scraped the azure sky and menacing shadows cloaked the hills. No one knew he was in trouble.

Up on the bank, something snapped. He tried to remember what he'd read about increasingly bold coyotes. A tragic image filled his head. When darkness fell, he'd be lying helpless. There would be a circle of coyotes, yellow eyes gleaming in the stark moonlight, crimson staining their canines. His true, red blood dripping from their grinning jaws.

A dark silhouette appeared at the rim of the ravine. Geoff heard a low snuffling and a clump of frozen snow rolled down. A black and hairy creature clambered down the bank.

Geoff pulled himself backward with his elbows. He was going to die right here, in the backwoods along the Ribstone Creek. They might not find his body until scavengers had torn it apart and scattered the bones. He passed out.

The setting sun streaked the sky with mauve and draped the hilltops in purple. It would be dark soon. Geoff woke as gentle hands probed his ankle. He opened his eyes to see a hairy, black Sasquatch. Golden eyes met his and the intelligence in their depths calmed him. The beast pulled his sock down to expose the swelling and bruising.

Big Foot's hands on his ankle should have had him screaming in pain. Instead, all he felt was a dull ache. Keeping his eyes on the Sasquatch, Geoff reached into the backpack for his camera. He turned it on and pointed it at the beast. Big Foot shook its shaggy head.

Geoff snapped the picture. The LED screen showed a perfect likeness. He'd done it! He had a picture that was clear proof of Big Foot's existence. In his excitement, he forgot to watch the Sasquatch, who grabbed the camera and removed the memory card. Deliberately, and keeping those yellow eyes on Geoff, he broke it between his thumb and index finger. There was a sharp snap and then he tossed the broken bits into the snow.

The sun lowered behind the hills and Geoff was terrified that the Sasquatch would kill him next. Instead, the Big Foot continued to watch him. Geoff got cold. The temperature was falling and he'd die of exposure.

Tears welled in Geoff's eyes. The whole idea had been a mistake and now, if the beast didn't kill him, hypothermia would. The Sasquatch shifted and scratched his hairy chest. Then he took Geoff's backpack and, rummaging through it, found one of the granola bars Aunt Gerda had put into the lunch. He unwrapped the snack and held it in one hand until it was warm. Then he gave it to Geoff.

Geoff had a bite while keeping his eyes on the beast. Big Foot stared back and waited while Geoff finished the granola bar. The Sasquatch smiled at him in the twilight, keeping his golden eyes on Geoff's. It was weird, but he felt so relaxed. He fell asleep, a deep dreamless sleep, the kind where breathing is slow and regular, and saliva pools to dribble from the corner of the mouth. With gentle fingers, the Sasquatch took Jeff's phone and put it out of reach. Then he shook Geoff's shoulder, but the young man slumbered on. Big Foot gathered him into his arms and strode through the ravine to the creek bed.

~ ~ ~

When Geoff woke, he was laying on a blanket near a blazing bonfire. Flames shot into the night air and cast grotesque shadows in the trees and shrubs. Geoff lifted his head. He could smell hot, spicy chili and roasting wieners. Someone helped him sit and Aunt Gerda handed him a steaming mug of coffee. He sipped it quickly. Warmth spread to his stomach and he drank again.

"What happened?" he asked. Aunt Gerda looked at him sadly.

"You found Big Foot," she said, and walked closer to the fire where groups of people were eating hot dogs. To his right, there were three women in lawn chairs. Uncle Hank added logs to the fire and sparks exploded into the darkness. To his left, a group of Sasquatch stood drinking beer and eating smokies.

He rubbed his eyes. The heated air from the fire distorted his vision. But it wasn't his eyes. There *were* Sasquatch, standing and visiting in their own group. Geoff struggled to remember what had happened.

"Here, Geoff, have a hot dog." One of the men handed him a bun stuffed with a flame-charred wiener. "Better eat a couple. You'll need your energy."

The party went on, but no one added more logs to the fire, and after a while, it died back into a bed of glowing coals. People drifted over to the ATVs, or started to put their skis on. The headlights of the quads crisscrossed the darkness as they drove up the hill. Geoff shivered in the cold.

"Uncle Hank," he called. "Are we going soon?"

"Soon," said Hank. "But you won't be coming with us."

Geoff attempted to stand. "Help me," he said. "I need help."

Uncle Hank wouldn't meet his eyes. "I'm sorry, boy," he said. "But this is the way it is. One of us is given to the Sasquatch to live with them. It's a guarantee that we keep their secret."

Aunt Gerda looked at him and quickly turned her eyes away. "Elsa knew it was our turn. You were the firstborn in the family. She should never have run away." Her face hardened and then she joined Hank on the ATV. He had strapped his skis to the front carrier and the two of them were ready to ride home.

Uncle Hank turned the throttle and the quad sprang forward. He and Gerda were swallowed by the night.

"No… wait." Geoff tried to get up. A twig snapped nearby and he jerked around to see what it was. "Nooo…"

Big Foot shook his head and put his index finger to his lips. Then he threw Geoff over his left shoulder and, with long strides, caught up to the main group of Sasquatch.

In the distance, coyotes howled and yipped. The dull glow of the fire faded altogether as they rounded a bend in the creek. Geoff squirmed and hit the Sasquatch. When there was no response, he gave up and hung helplessly down the beast's back as it carried him into the night.

THE NOIR THAT WASN'T
by Halli Lilburn

Why was this homeless guy sitting across the desk from me? I was used to rich snobs walking through my door, begging for protection from people like him. He stared at my tailored pant suit and pumps, awkwardly trying to straighten the lapel on his worn-out trench coat. Like he could brush away his dirty appearance and convince me to validate him.

"Listen," I said. "I don't do pro bono work. Unless you can give me a deposit, I'm afraid I can't help you."

His toothless mouth trembled with palsy and his whiskers branched off his face like wild oats. "You'll get your money, Miss Anaitis. I'm telling you, if you can protect me

273

and my assets you'll be rich."

What assets? By the look of this guy he didn't have much to offer. "What's the catch?" I asked.

"You have to get it all back first. All the money that was taken from me."

That piqued my interest. I did enjoy breaking through unbreakable security systems, especially if it ticked somebody off. Some richies feel safe hiding in a cocoon of gadgets and software, but they fool themselves. Their money is about as safe as if they walked around with a hundred-dollar bill dispenser strapped to their backs.

Alberta is made up of a lot of farmers and ranchers. We don't have much in the way of elite society, but we do have one major commodity: oil. The oil industry is huge and the people who can get their hands on it have a lot of power. My new client, whose name was Harold Buchannan, claimed he was a big wig or at least he used to be.

"I know I don't look it, but I was once a CEO of Prime One Industries," he said, making a move to spruce up his shredded collar, then scratched his jaw instead. "Mr. Philias Munroe swindled me out of millions of dollars. If you can get back what's owed me, you will get a one percent share."

I frowned. "I'm not one to gamble," I told him. "I could waste a lot of my valuable time and end up with nothing."

He smiled under a barbed wire moustache, "Or, if you succeed, you could walk away with a year-long vacation to the Bahamas."

I sized up my client. He looked miserable, like a mangy dog. Nothing about him suggested he used to be a millionaire. I gave him a test. "Two percent," I probed.

He didn't even flinch. "Done."

Even though I determined I couldn't trust the guy, I still took the job. I couldn't resist.

"How will I get a hold of you?" I asked, assuming he didn't have a cell phone, or a landline, for that matter.

His jaw trembled. He wouldn't answer.

I rolled my eyes and blew air into my bangs. "I have a couch over there." I pointed around the filing cabinets. "You can stay here."

I don't know why I was bending backwards for the guy, but I guess he needed sympathy from someone.

I live and breathe other people's problems and, in my town, people have a lot of them. Every man and woman feeds off each other's weakness. It all boils down to greed. I need, I need, I need. Break into my house and find out who's sleeping with my husband, be the queen's double in case that assassin comes back, hide all this money I've been laundering. Humans are screwed up and they keep me awfully busy.

My first task was to interview Munroe and see what I could find out. His house was in Parkridge Estates, the new subdivision beside the cemetery with mansions teetering on the edge of the coulees, a gated community of richies who could afford a new house when the hills slumped and pulled these ones down into the river valley. They said it was worth the view. Richies think they own everything, control everything. They could build their houses on the edge of a cliff and waste their equity. And why not build beside a graveyard? They could buy their way out of superstitions and bad luck.

I exited off Scenic Drive, pulled up to the gate and smiled into the camera. "Is Mr. Philias Munroe in?"

A woman's voice came through the speaker. "I'm sorry he's at the summer cottage in California, again. Who is this?"

Whoever was on the other end didn't sound happy about him being on holiday without her. My bet was I was talking to his wife. "My name is Miss Anaitis. I'm from the Herald. I'm doing a piece on wives of the rich and famous. Do you know—"

She cut me off. "This is Jenna Scott. I'm his wife."

"Oh." I feigned a sound of surprise. "Could I have a few moments of your time? I could—"

She cut me off again. "Yes, yes, come up."

The gate buzzed open and I smiled to myself as I pulled my SUV into her driveway.

"Where did you say you were from again?" The wife of Philias Munroe had a servant bring a tray of tea, but she insisted on pouring it herself.

"The Herald, Mrs. Munroe." I took the delicate china cup in my hand. I'm sure it was at least one hundred years old. The view out the front window was expansive. Each sharp ravine cut through the earth like a serrated knife. Wildflowers and a carpet of grass was backlit by a low hanging, golden sun. The entire front of the house was on stilts, making it easy to see the coulee to the west peppered in tombstones.

278

"Oh no, please don't call me that." The woman across from me sat poised with excellent posture and flawless makeup. "I never took my married name. Just call me Jenna."

"Okay, Jenna. Why did you keep your maiden name?" I asked.

"Simple," she said, as she blew across the top of her cup. "I didn't want to have any association with Phil's parents. They're… well it's hard to say anything nice. Plus, they're American. Not me, I'm a local girl. That's the only reason we still own property here, so I can be in my element. His parents can't stand the cold and the wind, which is fine with me, if they never visit. He says he travels down south because he's concerned for their health, but sometimes if I call, they sound like they didn't even know he was coming, and they cover for him, you know. They cough into the phone like they can feel the cold seeping through the line."

As the conversation progressed, I realized two things. Mz. Scott was lonely and in desperate need of company, no matter who it was, and second, it wouldn't take much to get the information I needed. She didn't care about the Herald, only that I was also female, so I must be compassionate and trustworthy. She rambled on and on about her life and how much she hated even the most insignificant things. My foot was most definitely in the door.

I let her blab for almost an hour, all the while sympathizing with the plight of the rich wife, before I steered the conversation my way. "Has your husband ever taken advantage of his powerful position at Prime One?"

She pursed her lips. "You mean, besides the prostitutes and the drinking and parties?" Her eyes darted back and forth like she was trying to decide what to tell me.

"I mean, did he step on feet to achieve his

high position?"

She faltered, staring into her tea cup. "Umm..."

"Do you know a man named Harold Buchannan?"

Her quick intake of breath told me she did.

"He used to be on the board of directors—"

"Yes, of course, I knew Harry. He was a good man. We were close." She sniffed. "We were engaged once."

Interesting. Stolen money and stolen girl. "What happened? Why did you break it off?"

"I would have married him, but... but I never got the chance. He died almost ten years ago."

My eyes went wide. I was good at doing my research, but it hadn't even occurred to me to check if my client was alive. That hobo in my office could be an identity thief. I kicked myself. "Do you have a photograph of Mr. Buchannan?" I asked. I needed verification.

"Oh no," she said. "Phil would never allow

me to keep something like that." She wiped her nose with her napkin. "I mean I tried, but he found it and ripped it up. What difference does it make now? I've moved on."

"Hm, I can see that." I took a sip of tea.

She copied my move, adding a shake of her head. "No, I don't think I can let you print any of this. It makes me look unfaithful."

Unfaithful to a dead man? I needed her on board, so I changed the subject. "You've been married how many years?"

"Eight."

"Any kids?"

"Too late for that."

She couldn't be more than forty. Did she really believe she was too old? I could guess who told her that. I've seen women get brainwashed by their husbands. They lose any independent thoughts or opinions, and believe whatever they are told. Munroe had some sort of weird grip on her and I didn't like it.

I bid farewell and raced back to my office to confirm her story.

I stared at the computer screen in disbelief. It displayed a pic of a happy couple smiling at each other with the caption Jenna and Harry 2007. He cleaned up nice. The next screen had the same picture with Jenna cut out of it. This time the headline read Prime One Loses Partner. Harold was staring at nothing, smiling with affection at a missing bride.

I read the article. Harold Bucannon met a tragic end only days after his engagement to Jenna Scott. He was killed when his car skidded off the edge of Scenic Drive and crashed on the embankment below. He was pronounced dead at the scene. Without a will, his assets go to his partner at Prime One Industries, Philias Munroe.

Even with the whiskers and filth I could see the similarities between my client and the so-called deceased Prime One partner, but apparently, no one saw the resemblance but me. Was his faked death a setup just to rob him of his fortune? How many people had Philias paid off to make this work? The coroner, the police, even his dentist would need to confirm matching teeth. Did anyone actually see the dental records? Harold had no parents and no siblings. How convenient that Munroe was called to ID the body. And who had Munroe really put in the morgue, if it wasn't Harold?

In the morning, I barged into my office, making as much noise as I could, to make sure Harold heard me. He was slouched on the couch, staring at the engagement announcement in the paper.

"The thing I don't understand is why you haven't tried to contact Jenna," I pressed. "I mean, come on, even if the whole world didn't believe who you were, she would."

He choked up a bit, but quickly sniffed the tears back into his face. "She won't see me. I've tried. For ten years I've tried."

"She knows you're alive?" I was shocked. That minx was feigning heartbreak over her lost love. "Let me get this straight. You've been in the city for ten years and you've never run into her at the grocery store? A restaurant?"

"Do I look like I buy groceries?" Harold's voice grew furious. "She won't answer if I call. If I go to the house, she won't open the gate. She knows who owns the money, she only cares about herself!" Spit flew out as he yelled.

I yelled back, "Calm down!" My hand instinctively went to my desk drawer, gripping the handle, but not opening it. I'd moved Betsy to the glove box of my car the minute I let Harold stay on the couch. It's fine, I told myself, I'm not going to need her. "I'm sure you're disappointed that I don't have your money yet, but is this really about getting revenge on Philias and Jenna?"

Harold sat back, shaking his head. "I saw

her once at the park on Canada Day. We were waiting for the fireworks to start. She had a blanket spread out. Kids with glow sticks were running around her, making her laugh. I ran up and grabbed her shoulders. 'Jenna! It's me. It's your Harry!' I wanted to hold her and never let go, but she screamed and pushed me way. She had a flashlight and tried to hit me, but I grabbed it and shook her hand until she let go. With the light shining in my face, I pleaded with her, 'Look at me. Look! Don't you know who I am?' But her eyes showed no recognition, like she saw only a stranger. She fell back and kicked me right here." He pointed to his chin. "Knocked out a tooth. I started bleeding on the blanket."

"That's when Phil showed up, running through the glowing crowd, yelling, 'What's going on?' He told me if I came near her again he would have me arrested. He gathered up the blanket and wrapped it round her like a cocoon and whisked her away. I haven't seen her since." Harold let tears dribble off his wobbling jaw.

If I didn't feel sorry for him before, I did now.

So maybe it was time to break bad. Philias Munroe and Prime One deserved a good dish of karma and I didn't mind shoving it down their throats. I had a tech buddy named Cindy who owed me a favour. She could hack into the accounting system at Prime One and change a few numbers. Harold turned down the idea.

"I haven't got a bank account," he protested.

"That's because you're dead," I said. "Maybe it's time to resurrect you."

His face drooped, head shaking, and I couldn't tell if he'd done it on purpose, or if it was the palsy.

"Why are you reluctant? It's the easiest way to get your money back. Cindy can manage it."

"It's illegal," he said.

"Listen, Buchannan. I'm not going to walk over to Prime One and say please. What are they gonna do? Complain to the cops?"

"To be honest, I don't care about the money. I just want Jenna back."

"What?" My mouth dropped open. "I am not here to fix your relationship. You hired me to get your money and that's what I'll do. Your personal life doesn't have anything to do with me. You go fix that yourself."

"I wasn't asking you to." Misery poured over Harold's face.

The situation reminded me of Wuthering Heights. Personally, I saw no point in moping around pining for someone. People weren't worth it. I know I wouldn't be.

The phone rang. "Hello?" I answered. "You've reached Anaitis Security Agency."

"Uh, I thought this was the Herald."

I knew the voice. "Mrs. Scott, how can I help you?"

Harold stiffened in his chair. He made a hand motion, signaling I wasn't supposed to mention him. I rolled my eyes.

"Philias came home. You wanted me to tell you."

"I'm on my way." I hung up. "Harold, you're coming with me."

"No. No, I can't. She kicked me. She told me she didn't know me."

"I don't care about your sob story. For me, this is only about the money." I pulled his arm until he followed me out the door.

The high sun and bright clouds reminded me of a harsh interrogation light, sending a stabbing pain behind my eyes. The wind blew across the river, making an ocean of grass ripple across the coulees.

I sped along Scenic Drive, up to Parkridge Estates. "The minute Jenna sees your face, she'll realize what Munroe is guilty of. Then I'll make him give back the toys he stole from you."

"How?" Harold asked.

"Betsy." I flipped open the glove box and pulled out my trusted magnum, hiding it inside my jacket.

"Dear Lord," he said, gripping onto the dash as I took a sharp corner.

The gate was open to Parkridge Estates and I drove right in. Jenna was waiting in the doorway when I pulled up to her house. It was easy to guess who the man behind her was. His salt and pepper beard framed his face like a robotic mask, trimmed to perfection. So were his eyebrows. They fanned out like each individual hair was set in place.

"You must be Miss Anaitis." His black suit looked expensive, but how was I to tell? He didn't wait for a reply. "You don't work for the Herald. Jenna should have figured that out."

Mrs. Scott took a step back, fidgeting with the buttons on her pencil skirt, but saying nothing.

"I'm not on the payroll, if that's what you mean, but they know who I am."

"Yes, I'm sure you've supplied them with many interesting stories."

"They also know me very well at the cop shop, but I'm hoping I won't need to call them."

"Indeed," he said, motioning for me to enter the house.

"I've brought someone you should meet." I motioned towards Harold who was quite a few steps behind me. I beckoned for him to move forward, but he stuck himself on the front lawn right where the cliff broke off down to the river and wouldn't move.

Philias had a blank stare, waiting impatiently for me to expose him. "Well?"

"Harold Buchannan," I said.

"What about him?" Philias asked.

"He's standing right there." I pointed.

Jenna gasped. "Harry's dead."

Philias smirked. "There's no one there."

I looked from Harold and back. "What, are you blind? Harold, come closer," I called.

He didn't budge. His sloppy brown clothes and hair shifted in the wind, but his body was still as a statue. He wasn't even breathing.

"Harold, what's wrong?" I moved closer. "You have to face these people. Find some strength and get over here."

"This woman is delusional," Philias said to Jenna.

"You, Mr. Munroe, are a fraud and a manipulator. You stole this man's money and his girl and I'm going to prove it," I yelled over my shoulder as I stepped towards Harold. If I had to pull him up to the house by his collar, I would, but the closer I got to him, something happened. I could no longer see his face. It blended in with his coat like he was made of wood. The tree behind him cast a shadow over his whole body. I slowed down, wondering why I hadn't noticed all the green leaves above his head.

In his head.

Coming out of his head. The head that wasn't there anymore. I reached out my hand to touch his shoulder and felt only bark. I looked around, wondering how I could have mistaken Harold for a tree. I called for him, touched the trunk again, pushing on it like it would somehow change back.

"This is ridiculous," I said, scratching my head.

"I'll say," Philias grumbled. "And you're trespassing, so remove yourself or I'll call the police."

I stood there like an idiot for another minute.

Jenna rubbed her manicured nails like she was bored.

"This isn't over," I huffed and stomped back to my car. I got in and slammed the door.

Maybe Harold ran off as soon as I pulled up. That must have been it. Well, he could deal with my wrath when he walked back to the office. I started down Scenic Drive, squealing the tires to get out of Parkridge Estates. I was mad, and I drove too fast when I was mad. The road hugged the steep embankment in sharp turns as it wound around the coulees. Before I got to the cemetery, as I rounded a corner, the figure of a man stood in the middle of the road. I saw his face and realized it was Harold. I slammed on the brakes, skidding closer and closer until—I couldn't stop in time. I hit him.

He didn't move. The hood of my car went right through him. Or he went through my car. The only impact was the kickback from the brakes, which sent my face into the steering wheel. The car was off the road, one tire jutting in mid-air. Dirt and rocks rolled down the cliff below. I cradled my head in my hands for a second before searching around wide-eyed for where Harold had gone. He was sitting shotgun.

"What the hell?" I exploded. "What is going

on?"

He sat in a trance with his face drooping and his hands dangling by his sides. Slowly, he spoke. "You can take me back now."

"Damn right," I said. I pulled the car back onto the road and headed for the cemetery.

NEVER LOSE YOUR DOG AGAIN
by Alex Chappell

They say pets grow to look like their owners, but that was never the case with Rexy and me.

I know, Rexy is no kind of name for a dog. But I was nineteen, living with my dad while my mom's latest marriage fell apart. They got me the dog to motivate me, by which they meant get me out of the house. It worked, though. Rexy was part retriever, part pit bull, and he had a big dopey smile and fat pink gums that nearly swallowed up his teeth. He liked to head butt me to get my attention, which was adorable for the first three years of his life. After that, he was massive enough that a head butt could make me lurch forward.

Whenever that happened, and I fell, Rexy would run in frantic circles around me, darting in to lick my face very thoroughly for about five seconds, then going back to running, rinse and repeat until I stood up. Next, he would put his head down on his front paws, cock his head, and look up at me repentantly. I'd have to pet him, or he'd sort of crawl forward, still in that position, following me around. When I did pet him, he'd spend a few seconds still feeling sorrowful and guilty, and then his big, dumb tongue would come flopping out with pure joy at being forgiven and he would spring to his feet and all would be well. It was adorable, but I felt bad that he got so down on himself, so I trained him to go for a leg lean instead. Easier to brace against.

Anyway, his name was T-Rex, I was nineteen, but my five-year-old half-sister had called him Rexy, and who's going to argue with Bella? Not me, that's for sure. She's a

297

good kid.

It was Bella who was there for a lot of it, actually. It was her summer break, and my dad and stepmom made a deal with me. Spend the summer fixing up the Bruce Peninsula cottage they'd inherited from Vivian, my stepmom's great-aunt, and look after Bella while they went on their tour of Rome, and they'd pay me a pretty decent amount of money.

Now, I want to clear up some misconceptions. I wasn't the nineteen-year-old sponging off his parents anymore, but I had just lost my job in a pretty competitive tech industry, and then had a suicide attempt. *Your trouble*, Vivian called it. She had been unsure, initially, about letting me stay with Bella, as though trying to kill myself made me a danger to everyone else. I may not have had much going for me, but even I was more responsible than to traumatize Bella or leave her to fend for herself.

As my father explained to her, a summer chilling with a twelve-year-old while refreshing all my high school shop class knowledge and getting the fresh air and exercise my therapist was always harping on, while also getting paid enough that I didn't have to go back into the crushing world of white-collar dronery would be nothing but good for me. I believe he hinted that by doing this, they would have fulfilled their parental obligation to me, since they didn't visit once the six weeks I was in the hospital.

~ ~ ~

Bella, Rexy, and I moved out to the sticks of southwestern Ontario. Bush country.

I would have called anything out in that area the sticks, to be honest. Sauble, Port Elgin, Tobomory, they were all places that made their money by capitalizing on the longing for green spaces from big-money people from Toronto or Ottawa. I wasn't a rich Toronto kid, though. I was born in Mississauga and had been living in KW, sharing a one-bedroom apartment with one of those guys who seemed to perpetually be one semester away from finishing his degree.

Born close enough to Toronto that I could both proudly and sullenly announce to co-workers and dates that I was from the GTA, but prevented from ever living the big city life by a depressing amount of student debt, I didn't need to get away to towns with less than 50,000 people.

This cottage wasn't in one of those towns. It wasn't in a town at all, but down some winding green backroads, probably ten minutes' drive from the nearest neighbour, and twenty from a place where I could buy a Red Bull.

We stopped at one of those local hardware stores that obviously used to be a Home

Hardware, but had been abandoned by the company, probably for not turning a profit. The parking lot of Field's Hardware was empty when we got there.

"Take Rexy for a walk," I told Bella, but a man in a plaid shirt, smoking a cigarette at the front door said, "There's no harm in a dog, if he's a good'un."

Bella looked at me, possibly to confirm Rexy was indeed a good'un. I nodded.

"Won't the owner mind?" asked Bella, a paragon of responsibility.

"I am the owner," said the man, flicking his cigarette into the parking lot, before tapping his square fingers on a name tag with owner, manager above his name.

I squinted at the tag. "Is that a joke?" I asked.

He frowned. "No matter what they tell you, you can make it in this life without handouts," he said. "I did my time working small jobs. Now, I own this business fair and square. No handouts."

I flushed. "No, I-I meant your name."

"Why would my name be a joke?" He said, with that stiff, offended dignity that these old farming types tend to have.

"Chester?" I said. "And this is your store? Your name is Chester Field?"

The man regarded me with level eyes.

"Chester Field. Like, like, chesterfield. The sofa?"

He walked inside.

"Gosh, Drew," said Bella. "Why do you have to be like that?"

"His name is fuckin'—sorry, freakin'—Chesterfield, Bells."

She shook her head. "No wonder Mom and Dad are so worried about you all the time," she informed me. "You're not normal." She patted my arm. "I'm actually really cool, though, in school. So, I can teach you how to talk to people."

I followed her and Rexy into the store,

embarrassed and wondering if it would have been better to go back to Inpatient.

When we checked out, Chesterfield asked, "Where you going?"

I told him the closest intersection to the cottage.

"Figured," he said. "Heard new people'd got it. Keep 'em close to the house." He nodded at Bella and Rexy, who were examining a display of gums. "Especially the dog."

I was a little taken aback by this, since you'd think the safety of a child would be top priority. "Are there bears or something? Because Rexy is a pit mix. He can handle himself. Or do you think he's going to like... eat some endangered wildlife?" I was a little offended. "He's not that kind of dog."

"Thought you said he'd handle hisself against a bear?"

"Well... well... only if the bear attacked first," I protested. Bella was right. I wasn't normal and had said the wrong thing in defence of my dog.

"By the by," he said. "I'm not worried about the dog so much. More you. Dogs can pick up bad habits. From the wild things."

The way he was talking was making me think he had some hidden agenda. It made me jumpy, but I also couldn't come out and ask about it, in case it was just paranoia. Probably that's what it was. I just needed to take some of the as-needed meds in the glove box.

I hurried Bella out of there, anyway.

I listened to the old man, though. Even though there was no fence, there was a clearly-defined backyard that had probably been kept meticulously neat before the old woman died, which was strange, considering how much work needed to be done on the house itself.

When Bella wasn't helping me, she was in the house or in the backyard, always within earshot. And Rexy stuck to me like glue.

I was trying not to burn through the as-needed medication too fast. I didn't take it every time I was on edge, and maybe I should have been taking it more, because things were weird. One day, while I was attempting to reattach an eavestrough, an icy wind came up, and nearly blew me off the ladder. My fingers, which were now fat and clumsy with cold, skittered across the metal of the gutter. I was tempted to grab, but knew in some instinctive animal part, that if I grabbed onto that eavestrough, it'd rip from the roof. So, I leaned my entire body weight hard into the roof, reached up, and planted my hands firmly on the shingle. No gust that strong came again, but I would have sworn it got below zero degrees. I'd worn a flannel shirt over my T-shirt, mostly to prevent sunburn, and I was grateful for it now. Still, for the half-hour I clung to the roof, afraid of another strong wind, I froze. Then, it died away, slowly at first, then with the odd sensation of complete silence.

"Freaky weather, eh Bells?" I said, coming in.

"What're you talking about?" she said, barely looking up from some internet quiz.

"Didn't you hear the wind? Or feel how cold it got?"

She looked up then. "It's boiling in here. I got the fan down from upstairs." She pointed at the large white fan, which roared like a jet engine.

"Look," I said, ripping off my sock.

She recoiled in dramatic preteen horror. "I'm not smelling your feet!"

I shook my head, and the sock. A light sprinkling of snow, formed from the sweat in my boot going cold, fell onto the carpet, where it quickly vanished into nothing more than a damp spot.

"See?"

Bella grimaced. "That's weird, Drew. But

306

look, I swear it's been warm in here all day. Are... are you okay?"

I needed to be okay, but I wasn't, as evidenced by the night I woke up in a cold sweat and had to move. Needed a walk. I tried pacing around the backyard and that didn't cut it. I was feeling frantic. My hands were shaking. I was jumpy. I tried—and failed—to unscrew the cap on the meds.

The only thing to do, my brain told me, is to walk it out. You know what you need to do.

It was almost like—like a food craving. Sure, you're not hungry, but you need that exact thing, right now, anyway. You're going to get a palpable sense of relief from doing it. Just fucking go.

But I wasn't an idiot. I wasn't going to go alone. I'd bring Rexy. My dad and stepmom may not have intended it, but Rexy was almost like a therapy dog. When he leaned his weight against my leg, all 120 lbs of him, I felt anchored to the world. Couldn't leave.

I didn't love the idea of leaving Bella, but I took my cell phone, left her a note, and locked all the doors behind me. Bears didn't unlock doors. Besides, it was Rexy I needed to worry about.

I was on edge, bolting down the long driveway, almost outrunning Rexy. He was being weird, he was being slow. He whined.

The moon was pretty bright. I thought I would need my phone's flashlight, but I didn't.

Maybe I should have had it, because even though I was still on a dirt path, I didn't think it was the driveway anymore. It had gotten thinner. Worse, we were in the trees.

Rexy whined again. He wasn't a dog who whined, as a general rule. He'd whined when the paramedics came—back then. I had locked myself in the bathroom so he wouldn't have to see, and I texted my stepmom to look after him. When the paramedics broke down the door and stuck the tube down my throat, he'd whined until we were out the door. That was the last time I had heard it. Maybe the only time.

It's cliché to say the hairs on the back of my neck stood up or any hackneyed phrase like that. If you say that to someone, they'll think you're trying to sound faux-spooky. But sometimes, your shoulders tightening, your breath catching, that feeling that something is just a little to your left—what else captures it but that sentence?

"Go back to Bella," I said to Rexy. "Whatever it is, I've got it, okay boy? Go home."

I'd said Rexy could fight off a bear, but that was tough talk from a Kitchener boy who'd never gotten personal with one. And I wasn't going to make my dog take down an animal like that. I hadn't been taking my meds right, and that'd made me panic. That's why Rexy was out here, and a good person would take responsibility.

I bared my teeth and snarled. Maybe I could scare this fucker off.

But then Rexy ripped from my grasp, and went tearing off into the woods.

"Rexy!" I screamed, and plunged after him.

I jumped pretty athletically over the twigs and roots and crossed my arms over my face so I wouldn't lose an eye. I wasn't sure whether I'd been running for an hour or ten minutes, when I broke through the trees and stumbled—

Into the backyard.

In the blazing sun.

I could have been running a while, but not that long.

"Hey, loser!" Bella was on a lawn chair, a pile of Freezie tubes beside her. "Where have you been all day, stupid?"

"What time is it?"

"I dunno, two, I think."

I'd been gone for approximately twelve hours.

310

"I think I lost time, Bells."

"What?"

"Like, an alien abduction."

"You think you were abducted by aliens?" She squeezed her Freezie so hard that a chunk of the coloured ice popped out and fell on the ground. "Drew, you are taking your medication, right?"

"No, yes! No, I don't think I was abducted by aliens. Yes, I'm taking my meds. Hallucinations aren't something I have, anyway."

Bella looked at me. Her eyes were wide and round and her lip was trembling. "Mom says that people with your troubles can get worse sometimes, and then you'll have a brain aneurysm and your head will essentially explode. She said that I should call..." She looked away.

"No, Bella, it's not—I'm fine, okay? I promise. I was out looking for Rexy and I lost track of time. That's all. I'm so sorry."

"Rexy?" said Bella. "But Rexy's been here since I woke up."

Rexy crawled out from beneath Bella's chair. He looked up at me, but something was wrong. If you have pets, you know their eyes carry messages, and if you have a dog who loves you as much as Rexy, you know there's a softness. And their mouth is often curved into a dopey smile.

Rexy's eyes looked like turned-off TV screens, a greenish tint, very slight, not containing anything, just reflecting. And his mouth...

Well, he looked hungry.

"When'd you wake up, Bells?"

"I dunno, like seven?"

Rexy's mouth widened like a jack-o'-lantern. A strand of drool hung off a lower incisor, trailing to the ground. Rexy was a drooler, sure, but he always panted. His tongue would loll comically out of his mouth, sideways, slipping between two teeth. Not today. Just that one spiderweb of spit. That big mouth.

I hadn't realised before, really—Rexy had sharp teeth.

Bella let the subject of my strange behaviour drop more easily than I might have, in her position. Perhaps she was used to me acting irrationally. You can never really tell how your mental illness looks to people who are outside of it. You're never outside yourself. Maybe it wasn't even that strange, and it was just the crippling anxiety whispering to me that something was very wrong.

Rexy sought me out less than usual. He wasn't sucking up to Bella, the way he sometimes did if he felt she might be a better source of food. He was just... distant, but he kept looking at me, these half smirks, or disdainful glances.

Now, I wasn't sure how to approach this. On the one hand, believing your formerly adoring dog has started to resent you and look down on you is the product of a troubled mind. Of all the things I could claim in this life, a troubled mind was certainly chief among them. The important thing to know about me is that I had unshakeable opinions about certain things. One of those things was the goodness of dogs.

See, people who don't like dogs will say dogs are dumb and, too often, dog owners make the mistake of saying, No, he's so smart, why did he—

But dogs are dumb. That's not a criticism. It's the best thing about them. Cats are smart. And that makes cats too human by far. Cats calculate. Cats scheme. A cat would backstab or betray you in a heartbeat.

Not so, a dog. The extra space that should go to a dog's brain is given to a dog's heart. A dog loves you unconditionally, just because they're too dumb to see the malice, the cruelty, the self-regard you are capable of. A dog loves, to quote a cheesy saying, like it's never been hurt.

My anxiety has given rise to many thoughts that people might hate me, or think less of me. Never a dog, and certainly, never Rexy.

I was up late fretting over it, when I heard the squeeeeeak. I got out of bed to see what was going on. Now, I'm not an idiot. I've seen horror movies, but I had a little sister and a dog to look after, and you can't cower in bed and let them get slaughtered. So, I went into the kitchen.

It was the back screen door, which was what I had thought. Rexy stood in the door frame, half-in and half-out, the screen door resting against one flank as he froze.

"Rexy," I hissed. Then, he bolted. The door slammed behind him. I rushed to it, flung it open, but the following squeeeeeak made me pause. Last night, I had gone tearing out and lost twelve hours. Left Bella alone. Now, either I was cracking up, or something was indeed rotten in the state of Denmark. Either way, the woods weren't the place for me, not to keep her safe.

As I went to the couch, preparing to sleep there in case I heard anything else, I couldn't stop one thought, on a loop like a model train. How did Rexy open the screen door?

The next morning, as Bella came into the living room, I said, oh-so-casually, "Hey, Bells. Remember to shut the heavy door at night, not just the screen door, okay?"

"Thanks," she said. "Because I look like an idiot."

"It was just open last night."

"Well, I didn't do it," she said. "Maybe you didn't close it when you let Rexy out to pee."

I didn't say anything, guilty.

"Doesn't he usually not go at night? And you took him out last night and now?" She walked over to the screen door and pushed it open. Despite giving Bella a hard time about leaving it open last night, I hadn't shut it after

Rexy left, just in case he came back.

Lo and behold, there was Rexy, trotting right through. I felt my heart jump in relief, but then, it stilled.

"Bells, does Rexy look... weird to you?"

"No, he just looks like your big, dumb, slobbery dog," she cooed, rubbing his back. "Who's a big, dumb, slobbery dog?"

That day, I couldn't have told you how he looked different. The next night, when I shut and deadbolted the back door, and he still got out, I couldn't have. The night after, when I vowed to stay up all night—and could swear I didn't fall asleep—and he still got past me, I still couldn't. Eventually, the change was noticeable enough to put into words. His brows were bony, ridged. His front half was bulkier than his back, ridiculously muscled. His tongue was black. His eyes were thickly glazed. He didn't breathe, he huffed—the gasps of a dying racehorse, and his gums were pulled back from incredibly sharp teeth.

Even Bella noticed. "Stop letting him out," she said. "He's getting mean."

"He has to go out," I said, hollowly. "I can't stop it."

The real kicker came our last night here. I'd gone back to the bedroom to sleep. No point being uncomfortable on the couch when it didn't do anything, but I'd gotten up for a glass of water. He probably wasn't expecting that. I think, if he knew I was awake, he could have avoided detection. Bella's door was open and, when I walked by, he was on Bella's bed. His teeth were bared and tiny chains of drool linked him to Bella's face. His mouth was so, so close to my baby sister.

You'd expect a dog displaying that sort of aggressive behaviour—

No.

You wouldn't expect that sort of behaviour in a dog, because it wasn't a prey drive, and it wasn't the attacking of a threat, and it wasn't a display of territory. It was menace. It

318

was a beast from hell savouring the last moment a little girl slept soundly, before he tore her apart. It was basking in the anticipation of savage violence. And that—that was not an animal behaviour.

Even if it had been, you'd expect a dog to be growling, but he was deadly silent. I knew, I knew, it was because he wanted the first bite to sink deep, his upper canine puncturing her eye, his lower jaw coming up through her chin. He wanted her to wake up like that, caught like an animal in a trap.

I lunged.

Thank God, he was still wearing his collar, because I got hold of that and pulled him off her. If he'd known I was coming, he could have braced himself against it, and probably snapped the collar—but he didn't. I think that sick fucking thing that my dog had become was too lost in the moment of ecstasy to really be aware of his surroundings. He hit his side hard.

I grabbed the lamp from Bella's bedside table and smashed it over his skull. He was still awake, breathing those heavy pants, but he wasn't getting up. I took the rug he had fallen on, raised the edges around him and dragged it out and—

You don't need to hear what happened next. There's no need. It gave me absolutely no pleasure. I believe, truly and sincerely that, if it had just been me and Rexy at the cottage, I would have let whatever happened, happen, rather than lift a finger against that dog, that good boy who leaned on my legs and loved me so much—but it was for Bella, and I was her big brother. So, I did what had to be done.

I didn't bury Rexy, but I took him down the driveway and a little way out into the woods, the place he'd first run off the path. I am convinced that he ran that day to lure something away from me, to keep me safe.

I built him a little cairn, to keep him

covered. I shouldn't say him, because, at the end, that wasn't my dog anymore. My dog had been gone a long time by that point. But he had been my dog, so...

When we loaded the car, Bella knew something wasn't right. Not hard. I was practically catatonic.

"What am I supposed to tell Mom and Dad?" she asked.

"About Rexy running away?"

"About you, Drew. You didn't even want to look for him."

"I did look, Bells."

She looked at me, and her big eyes were solemn. For once, she didn't tease me, or make some flippant little-sister comment. "Drew... will you think about going back to the hospital? I'm scared for you. I've been scared all summer, but now..." She started to cry a little.

"Hey, Bells. Hey, I'm okay." I hugged her. "That will definitely be something I talk to the doctor about, okay? I promise."

I really thought the hospital might be the best place for me. As we drove down that twisted driveway, I saw something that made me pull the car to the side of the road and peer into my mirror.

Then I floored it.

"What, Drew? What's going on?"

I didn't answer her.

I might be going back to the hospital just for help dealing with what I saw.

Like I said, dogs look like their owners, and Rexy never looked like me.

But that thing he morphed into this summer? The thing I pulled off my sister?

It looked a hell of a lot like the thing I saw in the woods by his grave.

ABOUT THE AUTHORS

Joan Baril

Author of Sisterhood

Joan M. Baril, a native of Thunder Bay, Ontario, is a short story writer with seventy-two pieces published mainly in Canadian literary magazines including Prairie Fire, Room, Wall-eye, The Antigonish Review, Canadian Forum, Herizons, Ten Stories High, The New Orphic Review and several collections of short stories. She has won many awards for her stories and was nominated for the Journey Prize by The Antigonish Review.

She leads an active literary life with a literary blog (http://literarythunderbay.blogspot.com) and a membership in several writing organizations. In 2015, the Northwestern Ontario Writer's Workshop awarded her the Khoui Award for "Outstanding contribution to the literature of Northwestern Ontario."

A

The Canadian Government presented her with a Citation for Citizenship listing "outstanding achievements" exemplifying "Canadian values" for her newspaper column on immigrant issues. She also writes a monthly gardening column for Thunder Bay Seniors.

Alex Chappell

Author of
Never Lose Your Dog Again

Alex has been telling stories since before she could speak - ask her grandmother. She is currently a grad student at the University of Western Ontario, where she received her BA with an Honors Specialization in English Literature and Creative Writing. Passionate about sharing literature with others, Alex has been involved in the selection committee of the literary magazine, The Rusty Toque, and has volunteered to teach youth to improve their reading skills.

C

Bronwynn Erskine

Author of
Rain, Drizzle and Fog

Bronwynn Erskine is a queer woman currently living in Newfoundland after escaping southern Ontario for the glorious Atlantic coast. She writes primarily fantasy with increasing forays into horror and soft science fiction, but has been threatening to write a western for some time now. Her publishing credits include short stories in a pair of anthologies from local Newfoundland publisher Engen Books (Chillers from the Rock and Flights from the Rock), and one in an upcoming anthology from Tyche Books (Air: Sylphs, Spirits, and Swan Maidens). When not writing she dabbles in acrylic and watercolour painting, and has begun attempting to grow a garden.

D

Brenda Fisk

Author of
The Right Thing

Brenda writes in a variety of genres including fiction, non-fiction and children's adventure. The Right Thing was the 2018 Northwest Ontario Writer's Workshop (NOWW) short story winner for creative nonfiction. Retired from policing, Brenda has the luxury to write when she feels like it and publishes work she feels passionate about. She enjoys working with wood, fixing things and kind of wishes she'd picked up more construction skills along the way.

Michael Foy

Author of
The Powderman

Michael was born and raised in Surrey, BC. He completed degrees in psychology and teaching at Simon Fraser University. He now lives and works in Montréal with his wife and two daughters. He has published stories in The Nashwaak Review, Grain Magazine, Blank Spaces, Literally Stories, QWERTY and The Impressment Gang. He is working on a manuscript of short fiction.

Allan Jones

Author of The Pilot

Allan Jones lives in Ontario with his wife Gill. He grew up in Merseyside, UK before studying chemistry at Bangor University in North Wales. After

F

periods living in Norfolk and London, he and his family moved to Canada. Most of his working career has been spent as a professional chemist.

A keen reader, on a business flight one day he had the thought, 'If this was my detective, I would…' The idea didn't leave and he began creative writing as retirement approached. Writing and publishing novels (and the occasional short story) are now among the most rewarding aspects of his working life. He is the author of (currently) a set of seven art crime novels (The Catrin Sayer Mysteries), featuring a Welsh police officer based in London, England. His most recent novel, Canons, is an investigation into the suspicious death of a priest, set initially in the English Lake District and later in a court of canon law, in Hamilton, Ontario.

Allison Gorner

Author of
Killer First Date

Before becoming a short story author and screenwriter, Allison has been a librarian, production assistant, art director, and coalminer. She has diplomas in Cinema, Television, Stage & Radio, and Writing for Children, and is a member of Alberta Romance Writers' Association (ARWA) and Calgary Society of Independent Filmmakers (CSIF). She finds time to write when she can extricate herself from her four kids and their pounding on the bathroom door.

H

Laurie Hodges Humble

Author of Friday Afternoon Deposit

When she's not conjuring up well-developed characters in unique plotlines often laced with humour, Laurie Hodges Humble is either reading a book in the sunniest room in the house or listening to an audio book while driving. She is a loyal fan of Coronation Street, prefers red wine to white wine, Smarties to M&M's, and has a sweet spot for Old English Sheepdogs. Her favourite tea is English Breakfast, which she drinks any time of day.

Having lived in all three western provinces, Laurie currently resides in a small Alberta town with her hubby and two spoiled cats.

As a proud Canadian she takes delight in slipping u's into certain words. Keeps everyone on their toes!

I

Halli Lilburn

Author of
The Noir That Wasn't

Halli Lilburn enjoys exploring many genres including speculative fiction, paranormal and horror. She is also a poet and a playwrite. She has works in Tesseracts 18: Wrestling with Gods, Teseracts 22: Alchemy and Artifacts, We Shall Be Monsters by Renaissance Press, Spirited by Leap Books, Carte Blanche, Vine Leaves, and many others. She is a structural editor with essentialedits.ca and an editor for The Dame Was Trouble by Coffin Hop Press. Her education includes Library Operations, Art History, Creative Writing, Music and Fashion Design. She is a librarian, artist and mother of three and resides in Lethbridge, Alberta.

J. McMullin

Author of Upstream

As a child, J. McMullin spent hours jumping on the trampoline and imagining elaborate stories. As an adult, J. spends hours reading case law and drafting legal documents.

One of these things is better than the other. Follow him on twitter: @JMwriteswords

Stacey O'Sullivan

Author of
The Weight of Lives

Stacey spends much of her time reading and creating art. She is a crazy cat lady who would rather pet cats than do anything else. A retired paramedic, she holds a Bachelor of Arts in Fine Arts and a Master's in Leadership with a Health Specialization.

K

Maria Morrison

Author of Wild Thing

Maria Morrison was born and raised in rural Nova Scotia's Annapolis Valley. She is 34 years old and lives with her partner and daughter in the Valley village of Bridgetown. Her works can be found scattered across various anthologies and collections worldwide, including Bareback Literature, The National Poetry Institute of Canada and Theories of HER. Maria can usually be found spending time with her daughter, giving quests to brave adventurers or scribbling madly in tiny notebooks. She is a community volunteer, diligent worker and proud mother.

John Pringle

*Author of
Northern Mallards*

John Pringle moved to northwestern Ontario when he was four years old and is forever grateful to his parents for such a wise choice. He has written and published four collections of short stories and has more to come. He lives in Atikokan, but spends much of his time at Nym Lake. His books are for sale in Thunder Bay and Atikokan, or by contacting him directly at jpringle@nwon.com

M

Robert Runté

Author of
Age of Miracles

Robert Runté, PhD, is Senior Editor with EssentialEdits.ca and was formerly Senior Editor for Five Rivers Publishing, a small Canadian press for which he acquired and edited 30 books, primarily science fiction and fantasy. A former professor, he has won three Aurora Awards (Canadian SF&F) for his literary criticism and is shortlisted again for 2020. In 2018, he inherited the incomplete manuscripts of Canadian SF&F author Dave Duncan to finish and publish. Robert's own fiction has been published in a variety of venues, and four of his short stories have been reprinted in "best of" collections.

N

Jack Shedden

Author of Iambic Heptameter and the Abduction of Muriel

Jack Shedden is an occasionally retired machinist who, between working on kids houses, rebuilding his 100+ year old cabin in Pearl, and spending time with grandkids, squeezes in a bit of writing. As a longtime member of the Thunder Bay Writers' Guild, and supporter of Northwestern Ontario Writers Workshop, he writes about the people and places he has met and visited. The stories are not always easy to read, some have dealt with the aftermath of fatalities witnessed in his 40 years working in heavy industry, some with drug abuse and its effect on families, and any everyday interaction with people he thinks deserve a story.

And, when the mood takes him, he likes to sneak in a little humour.

O

Linda White

Author of Family Ties

I live in a small town in rural Alberta with my husband and two dogs. I enjoy my retirement and its opportunities to socialize, write, read, and garden. The outdoors is one of my joys and I love walking my dogs and camping. Best of all is the time I can spend with my grandchildren. I write short stories, flash fiction, and have a novel in revision.

I maintain a blog at

http://box5400.temp.domains/~whatdok1/

www.ingramcontent.com/pod-product-compliance
Lightning Source LLC
Chambersburg PA
CBHW022246020726
47496CB00004B/1086